JOHN STEINBECK

THE LITERARY WEST SERIES

SAN FRANCISCO

JOHN STEINBECK

The California Years

BY BRIAN ST. PIERRE

CHRONICLE BOOKS

To Judy

Printed in the United States of America

LIBRARY OF CONGRESS CATALOGING IN
PUBLICATION DATA

St. Pierre, Brian.
John Steinbeck, the California Years.
(Literary West series)
Bibliography: p. 116.
Includes index.
1. Steinbeck, John, 1902–1968 –
Biography. 2. Steinbeck, John, 1902–
1968 – Homes and haunts – California.
3. Novelists, American – 20th century –
Biography. 4. California – Biography.
I. Title. II. Series.
PS3537.T3234Z8668 1983 813'.52 [B]
83-17186 ISBN 0-87701-281-4

PHOTO AND ILLUSTRATION CREDITS

The Valley Guild, Salinas: pages 10,
24, 28, 56, 64.

John Steinbeck Library, Salinas:
pages 17, 41, 48, 106, 110.

Federal Archives and Records Center,
San Bruno: pages 78, 93.

San Francisco *Chronicle*: page 88.

BOOK AND COVER DESIGN
Howard Jacobsen / Triad

COMPOSITION
Type by Design

EDITING
Linda Gunnarson

CHRONICLE BOOKS
870 Market Street
San Francisco, California 94102

CONTENTS

ACKNOWLEDGMENTS

Most of the research for this book
was conducted at the John Steinbeck
Library in Salinas, which has an
extensive collection of materials,
including the valuable Oral History
Project recorded by Pauline Pearson,
George Robinson, and others who
captured many of the recollections of
those who knew John and Carol
Steinbeck and Ed Ricketts, some of
whom are quoted herein. I wish to
pay special thanks to Librarian Mary
Gamble and Library Director John
Gross for their help. Additional
research was done at the Stanford
University Library and the San Francisco Public Library, whose belea-
guered staffs were invariably helpful.

Additional thanks to James P.
Delgado, who provided me with published articles and a thesis that clari-
fied important points, and to the late
Tom Collins, whose "Weekly Reports
of the Camp Manager" provide the
best picture imaginable of the day-to-
day life of the migrant workers; they
still deserve to be published.

Thanks also to Mrs. Elaine Steinbeck for permission to quote from published material of John Steinbeck.

PREFACE

CRANKY AND TIRED, JOHN
Steinbeck approached California warily in the late autumn of 1960.
He had been away a long time, had endured (and collaborated in) tu-
multuous times in public ways in that time, and was road-weary and
apprehensive about meeting friends and enemies alike at his destina-
tion. He had traveled around America mostly unrecognized and enjoyed the return of anonymity, but now he was returning to a place
where almost everybody knew him, had a strong opinion about him,
or both.

He lingered two days among the giants of the redwood country,
ruminating and catching his emotional breath, then took the plunge
and headed on south. The first step was the easiest. As he wrote in
Travels with Charley:

Once I knew the City very well, spent my attic days there, while others
were being a lost generation in Paris. I fledged in San Francisco, climbed
its hills, slept in its parks, worked on its docks, marched and shouted in
its revolts . . . It had been kind to me in the days of my poverty and it did
not resent my temporary solvency.

The next stop, the home country, was tough—and mean. Besides
the traditional welter of crosscut emotion involved in the return of

the prodigal, especially the successful one who has set himself apart, Steinbeck was very much a Democrat—an aquaintance of Eleanor and Franklin Roosevelt, friend of Adlai Stevenson, and rooter for John F. Kennedy—heading into the rockribbed Republican bosom of his family at the height of the Kennedy–Nixon election campaign. "I arrived in Monterey, and the fight began," he wrote. "A stranger hearing us would have called the police to prevent bloodshed."

Things got worse. He had a bibulous reunion with his old *paisano* friends at Johnny Garcia's bar in Monterey, and the embraces and endearments turned to edginess and anger on both sides as he explained why he'd been away and would go again:

Step into the street—strangers, foreigners, thousands of them. Look to the hills, a pigeon loft. Today I walked the length of Alvarado Street and back by the Calle Principal and I saw nothing but strangers. This afternoon I got lost in Peter's Gate. I went to the Field of Love back of Joe Duckworth's house by the Ball Park. It's a used-car lot. My nerves are jangled by traffic lights. Even the police are strangers, foreigners. I went to the Carmel Valley where once we could shoot a thirty-thirty in any direction. Now you couldn't shoot a marble knuckles down without wounding a foreigner . . . If this were my home, would I get lost in it? If this were my home could I walk the streets and hear no blessing?

Too many times, those who stay can only see leaving as a rejection, without any effort to understand what drives those who are wayward; Steinbeck backed out of the bar two steps ahead of a brawl, miles away from making himself understood.

He had avoided other old friends from the Bohemian days, but now he had got in touch and they had a party. Old crimes and triumphs were hashed over, "remember-the-times" batted about, and Steinbeck felt like an uneasy ghost, his attention wandering. "When I went away I had died," he wrote later.

The next morning, early, he fled. Webster Street, his lifelong close friend, slipped away with him and rode as far as Flagstaff, Arizona; they had more things to talk about, catch up on. In an interview later, Street recalled that the truck's engine was so noisy that they could hardly hear each other.

Leaving the Monterey area, Steinbeck made one last, important stop, at the top of Fremont's Peak, at 3169 feet the highest point in the immediate vicinity, to look back on the "long valley" he loved and chronicled. At any time of the day, in any season, it is beautiful there, a richly textured landscape of lightly muted color. "This solitary stone peak overlooks the whole of my childhood and youth," he wrote. "Here on these high rocks my memory myth repaired itself . . . I printed it once more on my eyes, south, west, and north, and then we hurried away from the permanent and changeless past . . ."

JOHN STEINBECK IN HIS FRONT YARD AND SUNDAY BEST.

John Steinbeck

I
THE NATIVE
SON

JOHN ERNST STEINBECK, JR.,

was born February 27, 1902, the third child and only son of John and Olive Steinbeck, in Salinas, one of a chain of agriculturally bound small towns that mark the flow of the Salinas River, and the only town in the area destined to become a city—a fact worth noting, because the tensions and pretensions of that growth had some effect on Steinbeck's later life.

Salinas was a town of about three thousand people then, lying on the cusp of a rich farmland whose chocolate-brown earth yielded a bounty of fruits and vegetables. The Spreckels sugar-beet fields and refineries just south of town added to its prosperity, and the Southern Pacific Railroad, running up through the heart of the valley and cleaving right through town and on to San Francisco, guaranteed it. Salinas had a goodly number of churches and schools, a fine wine merchant, an impressive city hall, some paved streets, a Masonic Lodge, a Chinatown, and a couple of decent whorehouses. It was a solid community.

John and Olive had arrived at this unlikely El Dorado after a great deal of peregrination, although neither's could begin to match those of their parents.

The author's paternal grandfather was born Johannes Adolph Grossteinbeck in 1839, near Dortmund in Germany; in 1856, on an Easter pilgrimage to Jerusalem, he met and married Almira Ann Dickson, of Massachusetts, daughter of a missionary. A few years later they emigrated to the United States and settled in St. Augustine, Florida, where Johannes changed his name to John Adolph Steinbeck, found work as a cabinetmaker, fathered John Ernst Steinbeck, and was drafted into the Confederate Army. As soon as the war was over, he moved his family north.

Leominster, Massachusetts, while undoubtedly more tranquil, did not offer John Adolph many opportunities for bettering himself, however, and he, like so many others in America, eventually went west (or "westering," as they called it then). He traveled overland to California and eventually settled in Hollister, a small town in the southern Santa Clara Valley, where he opened a grain-and-flour mill in 1874; he did well quickly, and his wife and now two sons joined him in time for Thanksgiving that year. The family prospered.

In 1890, John Ernst, then twenty-seven, moved down to King City, a bustling and somewhat rambunctious town that seemed to offer a young man some opportunity; he was a bookkeeper, and seems to have conformed to the solemn and steady stereotype of the profession. While living in King City, he somehow won the heart of Olive Hamilton, a smart and spunky woman of twenty-four who had been teaching in one-room schoolhouses around Monterey Country for seven years; some of the time she'd commuted on horseback.

Olive's father, Samuel Hamilton, was the sort of Irishman bound to become storied; as a young man, he had left the family farm near Londonderry and sailed around the Horn to California, followed soon after by his wife, Elizabeth, who took the easier route across Panama. They eventually settled on a homestead near King City, and Samuel added well-boring and blacksmithing to his farming achievements. He was known as a man of good looks, charm, and gaiety, a good neighbor and friend—and a successful man, too, with property holdings as far north as Salinas.

King City never fulfilled much of its early promise, and the climate can be fearful—a hot afternoon wind often blows there, keeping everything dry, dusty, and grim—so John Ernst and Olive moved down to Paso Robles, where he worked for the Southern Pacific flour mill. After the birth of their second daughter, in 1894, they settled permanently in Salinas, where John went to work for yet another flour mill.

It is impossible, of course, to know what dreams and aspirations John Ernst Steinbeck, Sr., had; he built a life of thorough respectability and quiet desperation according to his son in a letter he wrote to his publisher years after his father's death:

I remember his restlessness. It sometimes filled the house to a howling although he did not speak often . . . I think this was because he had abandoned his star in little duties and let his head go under in the swirl of family and money and responsibility . . . He was a man intensely disappointed in himself.

In 1899 Samuel Hamilton sold to his daughter Olive, for ten dollars in gold, a block of buildings on Main Street in Salinas that had cost him nearly two thousand dollars some years before. In one of the stores, John Ernst installed a feed-and-grain store. (He was no copywriter; one of his ads read: "PEEP! Yes, the peep of the chick is heard in the land, and if he is to survive he must be fed on STEINBECK'S CHICK FOOD.") Though not a great success, he was a good enough provider. In 1900 he bought the Victorian house on Central Avenue where his son and last daughter were born (and which still stands), and some years later was elected treasurer of Monterey County, a post he held for eleven years. He was thirty-nine years old when his son was born.

FEW MAJOR AMERICAN

authors have so assiduously mined their family and regional history as John Steinbeck; even in the brief account above, there are characters, themes, places, and dreams that appear and reappear in most of Steinbeck's best work—that of the California years. Morgan the pirate in *Cup of Gold*, handsome and glib like Samuel Hamilton, sails off to seek his fortune (and loves ladies named Elizabeth); the Wayne family and its stern patriarch travel west, overland, after the Civil War in *To a God Unknown*; schoolteachers figure prominently in *The Pastures of Heaven*; dour, uncommunicative fathers are recurrent figures (quite notably in *The Red Pony*; years later, long after his father had died, Steinbeck wrote its screenplay and added a plaintive line for the father: "Everyone calls me Mr. Tiflin—no one calls me by my first name!"). And, of course, they are all present, fleshed out in sympathetic detail, in *East of Eden*.

The California into which John Steinbeck was born right after the turn of the century was thriving. After a couple of decades of roller-coastering, the economy had settled on a healthy plane, diversified and stable; the railroads, sprawled across the entire country now, kept goods, money, and people flowing. A whole generation born in California — native sons — had been through the growing university system and were beginning to prosper; a real middle class was emerging and building value systems as well as businesses. California was no longer a rough and ready frontier.

The Steinbeck home on Central Avenue was a fortress of respectability, its Victorian frills and furbelows painted in modest shades of brown and blue. Olive Steinbeck took firm charge of her son's education early on, and the first book he learned thoroughly was the Bible, which she began teaching him at the age of three.

Both parents liked to read aloud — it was the principal source of their home entertainment — so John was exposed to a wide range of literature. When it came time for him to read aloud, though, he stumbled and lurched through the words, hemmed in by an overpowering shyness and self-consciousness, which remained with him most of his life.

John was a homely, jug-eared little boy, and lonely. His mother's considerable ambitions for him were frequently and bluntly stated, and living up to her demands at times seemed an impossibility; he actively hated going to school, where he of course earned good marks. The teacher's son could do no less.

When he was three, he was at least absolved of the responsibility of being the baby of the family, with the birth of his sister Mary. He responded by doting on her, and she became his constant companion, close friend, and first storytelling audience.

For his ninth birthday, John was given a copy of Malory's *Le Morte d'Arthur*. Writers usually remember the first book they owned with more than a little affection, but for Steinbeck it was an awakening, a magic carpet that lifted him up and away from drab and dreary Salinas and stultifying middle-class respectability; its archetypes and themes gave him a sense of a different order of things as well as keys to the world around him:

I was not frightened to find that there were evil knights, as well as noble ones. In my own town there were men who wore the clothes of virtue whom I knew to be bad. In pain or sorrow, or confusion, I went back to my magic book . . . If I could not choose my way at the crossroads of love and loyalty, neither could Lancelot. I could understand the darkness of Mordred because he was in me too.

After the Bible, Malory's book was the most important literary influence on Steinbeck's work, and at the end of his life, working for years to translate it into modern English became for him a talismanic quest, a search for his own personal grail.

He got the book, and much more, from his aunt, Molly Martin. She and her husband had a ranch south of Salinas, on the way to Monterey, in a lovely pocket valley know as Corral de Tierra, which he transformed later into *The Pastures of Heaven*. John spent many weekends there, decidedly a mixed blessing—on one hand, there was a fascinating landscape to explore and imagine in; on the other, the childless Aunt Molly was as determined as his mother that he would become an exemplar of culture; so she read to him and made him listen to recordings of opera.

A little while later, John acquired a friend—Max Wagner—who mattered a great deal then and later. Unlike John, Max was an extrovert; but he was also an outsider, by virtue of having been born and raised in Mexico, and had recently moved to Salinas. And so John heard firsthand about yet another exotic place; this one also fired his imagination and became an important part of his later work. As an added attraction, Max's mother had once met Robert Louis Stevenson, on the beach at Monterey. John was obviously enthralled with the story, for thirty years later he wrote an essay about the encounter.

The year he met Max, 1912, was a good one for John; that summer he was given a chestnut pony, which he named Jill. He was responsible for her care and feeding, and his father checked on him regularly. ("Nearly all his father's presents were given with reservations, which hampered their value somewhat"—*The Red Pony*.) Still, he and Max and Mary and another youngster, Glenn Graves (shyer even than John), enjoyed the gift immensely. The pony was stabled away from his house, and that winter was marked by heavy rains; it's easy to imagine the fears that ran through John's mind, since he set them down so well twenty-four years later. The next year he rode Jill in the rodeo parade, undoubtedly dreaming he was Arthur riding into Camelot (as indeed Jody did in the film version of *The Red Pony*).

With the acquisition of the "magic book," something else had been liberated in John: he became a storyteller and entertained his small circle of friends repeatedly. Sixty years later, in interviews, Max and Glenn both recalled the storytelling. According to Max, "Even as a kid, John was good at this. He was always interesting, and dramatized everything." Glenn recalled, "He could sit for an hour spinning out a yarn of adventure on the high seas or a tale of ghosts in an old mansion somewhere or a story about knights chasing dragons in the Middle Ages."

So John came out of his shell, though he behaved somewhat erratically and awkwardly, alternating quietude with mischief. He was now a voracious reader, and of adult literature—Hardy, Flaubert, Milton, George Eliot, Dostoyevsky—some of the same books his older sister Elizabeth was reading at college.

In high school, his storytelling and reading stood him in good stead; all his marks were good (though he needed some tutoring in math for a while), but he excelled in English. He also began to exhibit some of the traits that marked the man. Ora M. Cupp, his teacher for English composition and literature, recalled in a 1940 letter: "John was violent where a 'stuffed shirt' was concerned, and he didn't mind being loud or rude while he 'told the world' . . . He was likely to side with anyone that he thought was not getting a square deal, and to be noisy in delivering his views."

An interest in natural science also became apparent, something that deeply affected his life later. The father of one of his friends was an ornithologist, and John was fascinated by his collection of thousands of bird skins and eggs, all neatly filed and catalogued, and by his library. John's favorite teacher, Emma F. Hawkins, taught biology and made it fascinating to him.

His mother's efforts at cultural programming didn't abate, but John didn't mind the next phase: expeditions to San Francisco, where he saw and heard Duse in Ibsen's *Ghosts,* and Melba, Scotti, and Tetrazzini in concerts. It was a hundred-mile train ride then, and not especially comfortable, but he didn't mind. "When I was a child and we were going to the City," he recalled in *Travels with Char-*

ley, "I couldn't sleep for several nights before, out of bursting excitement."

The country was at war, Salinas was growing steadily, and the storyteller had secretly stepped up his ambitions. Late at night in his room, John was writing stories, which he sent out to magazines under false names, with no return address. He would then scan the magazines for months afterward, to see if they had printed them. "I wonder what I was thinking of? I was scared to death to get a rejection slip, but more, to get an acceptance."

He had also begun his nocturnal prowlings, so vividly captured in *East of Eden:* "I get restless at night – like an alley cat, I guess," says Cal, who was John's alter ego. "When I can't sleep I walk around to try to blot it out." As mild as the seamy side of Salinas may appear to us today, it was high adventure to John, and duly deposited in his literary bank.

In the spring of 1918, John fell terribly ill with pleuropneumonia, an infection and inflammation both inside and outside the lungs; he

JOHN, HIS SISTER MARY, AND JILL – "THE RED PONY."

was delirious and burned with a raging fever. In those days, surgery was the only cure, and it was eventually resorted to. The doctor came to the Steinbeck home and operated there, removing a rib and inserting a drain into the pleural cavity. The crisis passed and John began a slow recovery; he was left with a terrible scar.

He had missed most of the final quarter of his junior year and would have to make up the schoolwork in order to go on with his class. He did so with a will; something in the intensity of the illness and the nine weeks in bed recovering had changed him. He'd had a close call, and that's a good spur even for a boy, but more likely he was thinking of college and the opportunity it presented to get away from home and Salinas.

The aloofness that had characterized John earlier was muted in his senior year. He played basketball and competed on the track team, acted in the school play, was elected president of the senior class, and served as an editor of the school yearbook, *El Gabilan,* where his first published writing appeared, notable mostly because it foreshadowed the man's attitude as a writer:

The English room, which is just down the hall from the office, is the sanc-tuary of Shakespeare, the temple of Milton and Byron, and the terror of Freshmen. English is a kind of highbrow idea of the American language. A hard job is made of nothing at all and nothing at all is made of a hard job. It is in this room and this room alone, that the English language is spoken . . .

He applied to the college of his choice – spelling it "Standford" on a questionnaire – and was accepted.

The opportunity presented to John came with a reservation, as always: with four children to put through college, his father was unable to provide more than the necessities. John would have to work for walking-around money, and he was expected to justify the expense by succeeding in his studies.

Which he fully intended to do – he just had a very different defi-nition of "success," and it had nothing to do with the conformity he'd displayed in his senior year. He had no doubts; he was going to be-come a writer, whatever it took.

In fact, it took ten years.

2
THE AMATEUR
BOHEMIAN

AFTER A SUMMER OF HARD
work, Steinbeck entered Stanford University in October 1919; he
was seventeen years old, six feet tall, tanned, husky, and cocky.
Probably to satisfy his parents, he listed his career choices as teaching, journalism, and law.

Stanford University was a lovely pastoral campus in the town of
Palo Alto, with stucco buildings in the Mission style of architecture.
Prohibition was about to become the law of the land, but that would
have little effect on the campus, for Leland Stanford's widow was an
activist teetotaler who had willed much of the land to the university
on condition that it (which included much of what became the
town) be kept alcohol-free.

That was, however, the least of Steinbeck's problems. He was
among young men of rather more sophistication and standing, most
with courses of study laid out and career plans made, while he
floundered and burned with an ambition he didn't dare articulate
often or widely, especially since he looked like, and was taken for, a
bumptious rube from the country. His awkwardness and shyness
came crashing back, as did his self-defensive occasional rudeness. He
made attempts to fit in by going out for football and polo, but

couldn't make either team. (He did take a part-time job breaking and training the polo ponies, at which he was quite good, though he probably did not appreciate the irony of that.)

He chose as a roommate one of the first students he met, George Mors, in most respects his exact opposite; Mors was neat, organized, dressed well and studied hard. He was also blessed with an amiable and sunny disposition, however, and Steinbeck needed such a friend very badly.

It would be an understatement to say that Steinbeck didn't get on well at college—almost every aspect of college life brought out the worst in him. He found the academic discipline confining and stifling, and the stratified social life a frustrating puzzle into which he couldn't fit; during his time at Stanford, he never joined a fraternity or club (and was probably never asked). He took refuge again in defensive defiance and pranks, or withdrawal, spending most of his time reading in the library or taking long walks in the countryside.

In the beginning of his second quarter, he came down with a respiratory infection and took advantage of his parent's memory of the previous year's serious illness to drop out of school temporarily, somewhat amazed to find that he was homesick. He returned in the spring of 1920 and for a while made a strong effort to make up the work he'd missed and mend his ways. He also acquired another friend, Carlton "Duke" Sheffield, who was also secretly longing to become a writer but was not as rebellious about it as Steinbeck.

His efforts to catch up on schoolwork were lagging again when nature intervened, in the form of an appendicitis attack. Appendix and student were removed quickly, and he was soon once again a convalescent at home in Salinas.

His freshman record was miserable—he'd completed only three courses for ten units, hadn't gotten especially good grades even in those few, and had essentially accomplished nothing much at all.

That summer, Steinbeck and Mors worked as surveyor's helpers in Big Sur, where a link of the Pacific Coast Highway was being mapped. It was hard manual labor, especially clearing brush, and the food was terrible, with no nearby town for relief. After a few weeks, Steinbeck got word to his father, who lined up jobs for the young men at the Spreckels sugar factory near Salinas; Mors lived in the Steinbeck house and became a particular favorite of Mrs. Steinbeck, who saw in him a good influence for her errant son.

This put Mors in an awkward position, because Steinbeck didn't want to return to college and was trying to get some moral support from him; in the end, though, there simply was no choice for Steinbeck, nowhere else to go.

Back at Stanford, Steinbeck did not sign up for a full class load; he seems to have had a plan to mark time in college while finally getting his writing going, figuring that success at it would soften the blow of his never graduating and becoming a solid member of the respectable middle class. Within a short time he was ignoring his few classes for more reading, long walks, and late-night scribbling. Mors took time away from his studies to read the stories and comment on them, trying to help his friend in this desperate ploy.

It didn't come close to working. None of the stories amounted to anything, and there is no record that Steinbeck even attempted to have them published; additionally, his classwork was so atrocious that he was warned officially by the dean that he was on the verge of flunking out. His father had just been elected treasurer of Monterey County, an office in which he took great pride, and the young Steinbeck realized he was about to become a source of great sorrow and embarrassment to his family.

A wounded animal goes to ground. One night George Mors returned to their room at the dorm to find Steinbeck's clothes gone and a note on his desk: "Gone to China. John."

HE GOT AS FAR AS

San Francisco, where he made the rounds of hiring halls but could not get signed on a ship; he moved over to Oakland and clerked in a department store and later in a haberdashery. After a thoroughly miserable Christmas, he began to work his way south. He was eighteen, lonesome, and broke.

He stopped at George Mors' house in Los Gatos for a while and then moved on, working in the fields as a day laborer. It isn't clear whether he went home at this point, but it is likely, as he was soon working for Spreckels again, on its sprawling Willoughby Ranch near Chualar, a tiny town—little more than a glorified railroad siding—south of Salinas. The family embarrassment lived in a bunkhouse there, out of sight, if not out of his parents' minds.

Steinbeck had worked at a variety of jobs all through high school and had encountered quite a cross-section of humanity even before he was out of his teens. Much of the work was manual labor, frequently outdoors, and the experiences enriched his fiction and gave it authenticity and immediacy – at his best, which was often enough, he could skillfully convey just what it was like. His people were also vividly idiosyncratic, drawn from this wide gallery of observed characters.

The only problem for the would-be writer was that, at this stage of his life, he seemed to have no idea that he was storing up valuable information, or even that he would ever transform his experiences into fiction. According to both George Mors and Duke Sheffield, what he showed or read to them was a hodgepodge of tall tales, satires, fables, and adventure stories, as well as a fair amount of bawdy verse. Most young writers have begun the same way, but few have bet so much on such literary long shots.

Steinbeck worked at the Willoughby Ranch for four months, and worked hard, eventually becoming a straw boss, in charge of a small work crew. It was a lonely and exhausting sort of life there, and he left it before the hot summer began. He hadn't had much time or energy to write, and whatever thinking he'd done hadn't led to anything conclusive.

Back home in Salinas, he became a tattered layabout, ill-dressed and ill-mannered, wandering widely and mooning around like a second-rate parody of a Bohemian poet. His parents were puzzled, and the town was either amused or horrified; he seemed like a hair-shirted monk, parading his itches and scratches and guilt.

Steinbeck spent nearly a year in this wallow. Much of the time, he was in exile in his parents' summer cottage in Pacific Grove and also came to know Monterey in different ways from those he'd known as a boy. He was at ease with adults now, and Cannery Row was booming. During this time he wrote a great deal and, more importantly, began to write about the things he knew and observed. He also regained enough self-confidence after a while to submit a few stories for publication, though without success.

It was a terribly painful time; the things everyone else wanted him to do or be seemed to him terribly dreary prisons, and the thing he wanted most was probably the worst sort of folly. His failure was further dramatized in the spring of 1922 with the news that his younger sister, Mary, had been accepted to Stanford. The question

of his education, career, and future in general demanded some resolution now—he had been given an extraordinary amount of leeway
for the scion of an upper-middle-class German-Irish Episcopal family
in a small but thriving town. Enough was enough.

Stanford would take him back, though on a grade level more or
less that of a freshman; furthermore, he couldn't enroll until the beginning of the semester the following winter, when some dropouts
and dismissals would make room for him. Additionally, his father
would be financially pinched by putting two of them through college
at the same time, and John would have to work full-time until he
enrolled, so that he'd be less of a burden.

Steinbeck capitulated all around. The fact that he'd be close to
Mary, whom he adored, was one consolation; the fact that the job
his father arranged for him (bench chemist at a Spreckels factory, on
the night shift) gave him plenty of time to write was another. He was
giving in, but not giving up.

The fact that he was starting over at Stanford while his original
class was getting ready to graduate must have rankled; once again,
he mitigated the awkwardness of his position by choosing a good
roommate: Duke Sheffield, who was not only personable but a
would-be writer, ready to sympathize with Steinbeck's aims and
pain. Their previous acquaintance ripened into a friendship that was
lifelong.

Despite his earlier assurances, Steinbeck soon began his old
pattern, attending classes that suited him, taking long walks at odd
hours, and writing late at night. He paid enough attention in classes,
however, to pass all his courses, even getting a few A's.

That summer of 1923, he and Mary signed up for a zoology
course at Hopkins Marine Station, near the family cottage in Pacific
Grove, and Duke joined them for a while. Steinbeck was quite familiar with the lab, having hung around it as a child, and had even
cadged rides on the boats the students used for collecting specimens
around the bay.

Much has been made of Steinbeck's interest in marine biology,
and of its influence on his work, both good and bad, with many
critics inclining toward the latter. At this stage of his life, however,
it seems not to have been seminal. He liked and was fascinated by
science and, unlike so many artists, never shied away from study-

JOHN, HIS PARENTS, AND MARY AT HOME—READING WAS
A FAVORITE PASTIME.

ing it; on the other hand, he never got his highest marks in it either, and the interlude at Hopkins seems to have been more a way of getting out of Salinas than anything else.

Eventually the course ended, Duke went home to Long Beach, Mary went back to Stanford, and Steinbeck resumed his half-life of compromise, going back to the Spreckels lab for the first semester of the new school year. Officially, he was on leave from Stanford to earn some money and help his father with the financial burden of educating him; he'd resume classes in the winter term of 1924.

He was again working the slow and easy night shift. Duke had gotten a job on the evening shift of a newspaper in Long Beach, and the two friends seemed to put most of their energy into long, nightly correspondence. "They were, for the most part, less letters than literary experiments: dramatized incidents, essays, satires, discussions of political, artistic, or philosophical ideas, and not always serious," Sheffield later recalled. "His points of view were always fresh, his arguments original, and his treatments of the obvious full of surprises."

By the time Steinbeck resumed classes in January 1924, he had a new identity: the campus character. He dressed oddly (sometimes wearing a beret), smoked a pipe, and held forth sardonically in classes. He was also, of course, one of the oldest undergraduates on campus.

Now he roomed alone and bunched his classes early in the day so that he had as much time as possible to write. His friends were more or less the informal literary set. One was Frank Fenton, an associate editor of the Stanford *Spectator*. Upon him fell the burden of listening to the stories and ideas that poured out of Steinbeck, but he saw something in them and soon had him published.

The first story, "Fingers of Cloud," appeared in the February 1924 *Spectator* and seems now to be not much vindication for all the travail that preceded it. The story is of a dimwitted girl, a run-away, who takes up with a Filipino ranch hand. As terrible as their lives are, the two are better off together than they would be apart—at least it seems that way in the beginning. But the girl dis-covers that the man keeps the heads of dead horses in their rain barrel, and he won't abandon the practice, so she leaves him. The story could be an allegory for overweening religious conviction, or an attempt by Steinbeck to shock his readers, or merely the desperate attempt of a novice writer to find an ending for what is essentially a mood piece.

"In all my life, I've never known anyone else to concentrate so deeply on writing or work so hard at writing as John," recalled Fenton later in a career as a distinguished educator. He recommen-ded several other of Steinbeck's stories for publication, but only "Adventures in Arcademy," an overblown, allegorical burlesque of college life subtitled "A Dreamlike Journey into the Ridiculous," made it into print. Several of the others dealt with settings taken from Steinbeck's work experiences, but not realistically—he hadn't found a way yet to trust his material, to let it simply be and say what it was without romanticizing it. During this term, however, important changes were to occur.

3
"REPEATED, UNAIDED STRUGGLES"

EDITH RONALD MIRRIELEES

taught a popular course in short-story writing at Stanford for many years; Steinbeck had languished on the waiting list and was now admitted. Mirrielees was an extraordinarily gifted teacher, and she made a considerable impact on Steinbeck's life and art.

She was bluntly realistic and taught discipline as much as anything else. Two of her tenets, passed along early in the game, were that writing can never be other than a lonely business, and that the only way to write a good story is to sit down and write a good story. She made her students state their story ideas in one clear sentence, on the theory that that was the best way for a writer to be sure of what he or she wanted to say. She encouraged them to write at all times—but to be sure the writings had a point, always.

Many of her principles have become well known, as they should, being so sound; nearly forty years after this time, she published a wonderful book of her lessons. Steinbeck, by then her most famous former pupil, wrote the introduction:

If I had expected to be discovered in a full bloom of excellence, the grades you gave my efforts quickly disillusioned me. And if I felt unjustly criti-

---

John Steinbeck

cized, the judgements of editors for many years afterwards upheld your side, not mine. The low grades on my college stories were echoed in the rejection slips.

Once a storyteller, always a storyteller, and a sentimental one at that; Steinbeck in fact got an A in Mirrielees' class and was encouraged by her to keep trying.

Another important thing that happened in her class was the friendship he formed with Webster "Toby" Street, who became a close lifelong friend. Although destined to become a lawyer, Street was at that time hoping to be a playwright. Carl Wilhelmson, whom Street recalled recently as "a Finn trying to write like Joseph Conrad," was another valued friend from the class. The three went to meetings of the English Club, conducted on Sundays by another English teacher, Margery Bailey; the format was readings, discussions, and tea, the tone genteel and sophisticated. Steinbeck, of course, was disruptive, subversive, and sardonic.

During this semester, Steinbeck wrote half a dozen short stories, and one of them, although unpublished, was most important for him. Titled "A Lady in Infra-Red," it was a tale of Henry Morgan, the pirate, and it seems to have proven to Edith Mirrielees that Steinbeck had the right stuff. She encouraged him to polish it further and try to publish it.

Steinbeck finished the semester with good marks and went off to work at yet another Spreckels plant in Manteca, in the great and hot San Joaquin Valley, as dreadful a place now as then. Duke Sheffield joined him, and the two lasted a month before escaping to San Francisco, where they had a fine time spending their pay.

Still ambivalent about school, and now fired up by the encouragement of Miss Mirrielees, John again skipped the fall semester, but this time he moved to Long Beach and lived with Duke's family. They wrote stories at a furious rate, separately and together, and mailed them off to magazines in New York. They came back so fast that Steinbeck swore they'd been intercepted in the Midwest. To pay their board and molify Duke's parents, they took a job stuffing many thousands of envelopes with Christmas seals. That done, John went home, leaving Duke a souvenir of their adventure – a fat envelope of rejection slips.

Perhaps this experience convinced his father that Steinbeck might now abandon the dream and settle down, for he subsidized the

HAVING DECIDED TO BE A WRITER, JOHN DRESSED AS HE
THOUGHT ONE SHOULD LOOK.

resumption of tuition of Stanford again that winter. John's already
pinched lifestyle was cut back even further, however. He rented a
tiny shack behind a large house on Francisquito Creek in Palo Alto,
instead of living at a dormitory; Toby Street remembers it as a former
chicken coop.

The arrangement came about through the intercession of
Elizabeth Smith, an attractive divorcee at whose nearby home the
English Club had met several times. She was a newspaper columnist
and short-story writer of note, though she usually published under
the names "E.C.A. Smith," "John Breck," or "John Benton." She became
Steinbeck's mentor and goad.

Steinbeck had decided to try to expand "A Lady in Infra-Red"
into a novel, and Smith was supportive, even to the point of sending
her seventeen-year-old daughter to the shack every morning with hot
coffee and a little breakfast so he wouldn't have to interrupt his labors
until it was time for his first class. Caught up in the project as he was, it

soon didn't matter when the first class of the day, or any other, started — he was working hard full-time, scribbling in a minuscule hand in a bookkeeper's ledger his father had donated to the cause.

In her book, *Story Writing,* Edith Mirrielees wrote (and must have told her classes): "Only by repeated, unaided struggles to shape his yet unwritten material to his own purpose does a beginner grow into a writer." Now Steinbeck knew just what she had meant.

After a few weeks, he was called on the carpet at Stanford, in academic jeopardy again. He turned his crammed ledger over to Elizabeth Smith's daughter for typing and settled down to his studies, ending the semester with decent marks and a determination to give up on college. He was twenty-three years old, watching yet another class graduate without him and more friends getting married and setting out on careers. He, who worked so hard at his writing, was running the risk of being perceived as merely the campus Bohemian, an idler sponging off his parents, afraid to face the real world outside the safe haven of the campus. He knew what he wanted to do with his life, more than ever, and it was time to simply get on with it.

4
LOVE AND
PAIN IN
NEW YORK

STEINBECK DIDN'T LINGER
in Salinas after breaking the news to his parents, but pushed on to
Pacific Grove, where he settled into the family cottage and the business of finishing the novel—then titled *The Pot of Gold* —an ironic
commentary on the dreams of Henry Morgan and, perhaps, his own.
Writing became an even lonelier and more difficult struggle than
ever before, and it did not improve as summer eased into autumn and
"the Morgan thing" didn't resolve itself into a good book.

Having burned his bridges, the would-be author had no choice
but to go forward—to New York, America's literary center. His
sister Elizabeth had settled there, and some Stanford pals were already making careers there, so he wouldn't be all alone while making
a fresh start, and perhaps making something good happen. He
arranged a working berth on a freighter, the *Katrina,* which sailed
from Wilmington, in southern California, in early November 1925.

There are few things more exhilarating for a young man, especially a would-be writer, than going to sea, even if it is only for a few
weeks; sea voyages give the traveler time to relax, think, and especially dream. Stops in Panama and Havana, capitals of unbounded

hedonism, gave the trip more than a dash of adventure, although they also severely depleted Steinbeck's hundred-dollar grubstake.

There are only hints of Henry Morgan's Panama available to the modern traveler, unless he has the time and patience to stray and wander and poke around away from the bazaars and fleshpots of its cities, and there is no evidence Steinbeck did so. But the trip through the Panama Canal, with the jungle crowding down to its banks, provides a marvelous close-up of what is still some of the most impenetrable terrain in the world, and the descriptions of the pirates' jungle trek to the city in *Cup of Gold* prove that Steinbeck was paying attention.

New York City, of course, was a brutal shock after the sunny, sensuous pleasures and climate of the Caribbean. "It horrified me," he wrote in an article about the experience several years later. "There was something monstrous about it – the tall buildings looming to the sky and the lights shining through the falling snow. I crept ashore – frightened and cold and with a touch of panic in my stomach."

There wasn't room to stay with his sister and brother-in-law, so he borrowed thirty dollars from them and rented an apartment on Fort Greene Place, across the river in Brooklyn, and, as such, cheap. He got a job as a laborer pushing wheelbarrows full of cement all day long, helping build Madison Square Garden. He spent a mind-and muscle-numbing month or so of nothing but work and sleep.

During his stay in New York, Steinbeck seems to have made no effort to plug into the literary life. Most writers coming to New York headed immediately for Greenwich Village, to plunge into the literary and artistic ferment that have always marked the place. He was still the stubborn and insecure outsider, perhaps afraid, as he had been in the beginning at Stanford, of being seen as a rube. Since New Yorkers are quicker and better at that than anyone, he may have been right to keep to himself.

In February of 1926, just before his twenty-fourth birthday, Steinbeck got lucky: his rich uncle, Joe Hamilton, came to New York. "He was an advertising man with connections everywhere. He was fabulous. He stayed in a suite at the Commodore, ordered drinks or coffee sent up any time he wanted, sent telegrams even if they weren't important."

Uncle Joe tried to talk John into diverting his literary ambitions into the writing of advertising copy, but Steinbeck would have none of it; so Joe did the next best thing and got him a job as a cub reporter on the *New York American,* a quintessential Hearst newspaper noted for its breathless, slam-bang style of reporting.

He lasted a month as a general-assignment reporter: "They gave me stories to cover in Queens and Brooklyn and I would get lost and spend hours trying to find my way back. I couldn't learn to steal a picture from a desk when a bereaved family refused to be photographed and I invariably got emotionally involved and tried to kill the whole story in order to save the subject." He also wrote his stories in a highly individualistic, impressionistic style that necessitated constant rewriting by the copy editors. He was transferred to a beat covering the Federal Courts, downtown. At least he couldn't get lost covering stories.

It wasn't a job for an inexperienced reporter, but Steinbeck managed to muddle through for a while, helped greatly by older reporters for other papers who took pity on him. His salary of twenty-five dollars a week gave him some security, and the job gave him time and energy to resume writing.

He was encouraged in this by Amasa "Ted" Miller, an old friend from Stanford. Miller was an aspiring—and very proper—young lawyer with a deep affection for literature and for Steinbeck. He had friends in publishing and had offered to introduce the newcomer around, but Steinbeck demurred at first, still insecure.

Then, abruptly, his horizons broadened. Whatever his range of sexual experience up till now (and there are a great many colorful and contradictory accounts), Steinbeck fell in love, and it was a great fall. Her name was Mary Ardath; she was a showgirl in the Greenwich Village Follies and by all accounts a great beauty. John soon discovered that Manhattan is a great backdrop for romance. Mary lived on Gramercy Park; so he moved to that lovely neighborhood, to a seven-dollar-a-week room in a sixth-floor walkup at the Parkwood Hotel, and they had what he called "a golden romance."

Even love couldn't alter Steinbeck's plans or mitigate his stubborness, however. Mary was a sensible girl who didn't intend to spend her life supporting a fiction writer, and she urged him to get a good job as an advertising copywriter so they could get married and live comfortably. He refused; even then, he was stealing time away from Mr. Hearst for his own work. Mary left him and married a banker from the Midwest. To make things worse, he got fired from the newspaper a few days after she left.

"And now at last the city moved in on me and scared me to death," Steinbeck wrote. He looked for another job, peddled a few freelance articles to newspapers, worked at day labor, and fought off despair. Through it all, as ever, he wrote.

One friend Steinbeck had made through Ted Miller was an art-ist and book illustrator named Mahlon Blaine, who had encouraged Steinbeck and even lent him money from time to time. He also opened the door for him at a publishing house, Robert M. McBride & Company.

Guy Holt, an editor at McBride, had liked Steinbeck's stories enough to suggest that if the initial batch were polished up and sup-plemented by half a dozen more of like quality, he'd publish them. After the twin shocks of being fired and losing Mary subsided, Steinbeck buckled down to the project.

Soon he had the stories completed and proudly bore them to the offices of McBride, only to find that Holt had gone to another pub-lishing house, John Day & Company. Since he felt he had a verbal commitment from McBride, he submitted the stories anyway, only to be quickly informed that they did not meet the company's literary standards. He then sought out Holt at John Day, only to find that the house, always a very conservative one, had no interest in pub-lishing fiction by unknown authors.

Every writer has experiences like that, just the sort of thing that Edith Mirrielees had specifically warned about at Stanford. Still, al-though a writer may expect to have an adversary relationship with most of the world, he rarely expects that the phenomenon will extend to what he thinks of as a haven – a publishing house – and the shock of the discovery is brutal.

Steinbeck had had more than enough; as he later said, New York had beaten the pants off him. He went looking for a ship, found another workaway, and, in the summer of 1926, sailed home.

5
TWO LADIES, A LAKE, AND A CUP

STEINBECK TURNED UP ON
the Stanford campus one day shortly after his return to California, surprising and delighting Duke Sheffield, who had returned as a graduate student. Sheffield promptly took the threadbare prodigal into his house.

There was a pall over the reunion, however, and it illustrates something about Steinbeck's character and writing. Sheffield had recently gotten married, and Steinbeck had written his wife a snotty and vindictive letter from New York that is almost a parody of male bonding. "I love this person so much," he wrote, "that I would cut your charming throat should you interfere seriously with his happiness or his manifest future. You have in your hands the seeds of a very great genius, be careful how you nourish them." It romanticized their relationship – "We fought bloodily and the matter was strengthened," he wrote, when actually they'd sparred, with boxing gloves on, in the Stanford dorm – and bullied the girl: "I shall regard any attempt at alienation as an act harmful to him, because I know that I am necessary to him as he is necessary to me."

Needless to say, Steinbeck's visit was brief.

Much has been made of the fact that in Steinbeck's fiction there are very few happy relationships between men and women and, further, very few sympathetic women other than mothers or whores. Some of his attitudes can be attributed to his immaturity and the times—young men used to think and talk in the way he did to Ruth Sheffield—but a good deal of this dark view of women persisted to the end.

Steinbeck made his way to the Lake Tahoe area and looked up Toby Street, who had also married and was working at the lodge at Fallen Leaf Lake, nearby, during the summer vacation from Stanford. Street's mother-in-law owned the place, so it was easy to secure Steinbeck a job.

Understandably, he fell in love with the spectacular scenery of the High Sierra, and as his bruised psyche began to mend he started to write again. Street was working hard on a play, and the two buttressed each other's ambitions to the point that when the summer ended Street skipped the autumn session at Stanford to try and finish his play. Steinbeck got a job as caretaker for the home of Alice Brigham, widow of a San Francisco surgeon; he lived in a tiny stone cottage on the grounds of the beautiful house on the lakefront.

At first, it was close to an ideal life; he secured the Brigham house for the coming winter, chopped wood for himself, took long walks in the woods, and primed himself for the task of starting over as a writer. But once Toby Street and his family had gone for the winter, along with most of the other residents of the area, the loneliness and difficulty of the task set in, and he spent more time on correspondence than anything else, a scared kid afraid he'd bitten off more than he could possibly ever chew, alternating between self-pity and stoicism.

He had dusted off some of his early Stanford stories, polished them, and sent them to magazines once again, and during this winter he finally got a check instead of a rejection; it was only for fifteen dollars, but it made him a professional and happy.

The short story was called "The Gifts of Iban" and appeared under the pseudonym "John Stern" in the first issue of a magazine titled *The Smoker's Companion*. The magazine didn't last much longer than the money Steinbeck got for the story, which is an allegorical fable set in a forest fairyland. It tells of a song-maker named

Iban who seduces and marries the beautiful Cantha (promised to a rich man) with the promise of gold (the sun) and silver (the moon) and songs and eternal love. Cantha's mother convinces her that she's been duped, and Cantha breaks Iban's heart by leaving him for greener forests and realer gold.

The story immediately reminds a reader of Steinbeck's situation in New York with Mary Ardath, but it probably had applications quite as personal from earlier in his life, just as it has in the fiction of poor-but-honest artists for centuries. At any rate, he was at least following the dictates of Edith Mirrielees and writing about what he knew, however awkwardly.

During the winter, he also made a friend, yet another in the procession of amiable, fun-loving men he seemed to need to counterbalance his pessimistic, dour nature. Lloyd Shebley had arrived to work at a nearby trout hatchery (the lake was restocked every year by the State Department of Fish and Game). They visited often, and Steinbeck's interest in marine biology was reawakened as he helped Shebley with his chores.

Perhaps encouraged by the publication of his story, Steinbeck took up the Morgan novel seriously, starting fresh and working hard on it through the spring. He got through his light summer chores easily and was treated as a member of the family by the Brighams, endearing himself by tutoring the children and telling them ghost stories at night. The time passed quickly, and his output of correspondence slackened as his energy went into the novel.

Loneliness almost caught up with him the second winter, but he was better prepared for it. Shebley had moved to a larger hatchery at the far end of the lake, and Steinbeck's only company was a small phonograph. The writing went well however.

Finally, at the end of January 1928, he finished the novel; he put it aside, drained. Three weeks later, just before his twenty-sixth birthday, he read it through and thought it was an utter failure. In a letter announcing it, he wrote: "Isn't it a shame, Duke, that a thing which has as many indubitably fine things in it as my *Cup of Gold,* should be, as a whole, utterly worthless? It is a sorrowful matter to me." The letter is ponderously melodramatic, but at that low point, after a great deal of hard work and hardship, he'd earned the right. He concluded, as much of himself as his hero, "Goodbye, Henry. I thought you were heroic, but you are only, as was said of you, a bab-bler of words and rather clumsy about it."

He couldn't wait for the winter to be over, to move on again, get solid ground under his feet, and be around people. A sudden blizzard helped ease the way by dumping tons of snow on the area and col-lapsing the roof of the Brighams' house. Although there wasn't much he could have done to prevent it, he took advantage of the general distress over the calamity to terminate the job and the relationship, and moved on.

He had bought a battered, ten-year-old Dodge for forty dollars, and he drove around to visit Lloyd Shebley. Immediately, an expedi-tion to San Francisco was organized, and the two young men ca-roused until their money ran out, though not before they'd each bought a new suit. Shebley also hired Steinbeck to become his new assistant at the Tahoe hatchery.

STEINBECK HAD HAD

second thoughts about *Cup of Gold,* helped by Duke Sheffield's favorable opinion of it, and once he settled down at the Tahoe hatch-ery he began laboriously typing it from his handwritten ledger. The duties of looking after the trout fingerlings weren't onerous, but since the hatchery was open to visitors and a popular spot, his days were full.

Shebley was often away, and Steinbeck frequently had the task of conducting tours and answering questions. It was a perfect outlet for his deadpan humor and love of tall tales; he made up what he didn't know, which was considerable, and things became even more interesting after he put up a sign by the office announcing that he was a "piscatorial obstetrician."

One day two attractive young women, vacationing in the area, came to visit, and Steinbeck put on one of his better shows. That night he and Lloyd took them out, wearing their new suits. Stein-beck's date was Carol Henning, a vivacious and pretty twenty-two-year-old secretary from San Jose who was then living in San Francisco. Her sister Idell was Lloyd's date.

Steinbeck was a poor typist and had made little progress on a cleaned-up manuscript of *Cup of Gold;* Carol soon took over the job, and by the end of her vacation the project was done. She typed during the day, so for the first time in years, Steinbeck had his nights free. By all accounts, they danced in every speakeasy around the lake. Steinbeck perhaps fell in love reluctantly, still worried about his ability to make a living, but Carol was not so worried about it—she never seemed to have doubted that he'd make it.

Steinbeck mailed the manuscript to his old friend Ted Miller in New York, who had volunteered to find a publisher for it, and when the summer and the job ended, Steinbeck headed back to the cottage in Pacific Grove to start another novel. He went there by way of San Francisco, where he visited Carol. He didn't stay long, however.

It is testimony to, at the very least, his stubbornness that Steinbeck continued on with his dream. It had been nearly nine years since he'd decided to be a writer, he had devoted most of his time to scribbling away at it, and by this point had published a total of three poems and three short stories, only one for pay. Very few people had actively encouraged him.

Further, the pursuit of his dream had left him singularly alone much of the time, as well as undernourished. Few artists actively embrace solitude and suffering, knowing it will come to them unbidden, with the territory; most don't expect that it will last as long or cut as deep as it usually does, and quite a few give up or at least compromise. Steinbeck isn't unique in the ways he hung on and held up during his self-imposed ordeal, but he is certainly rare.

The new novel he began writing was a gift. Toby Street had given up struggling with the play he'd been working on for several years and had passed it on to Steinbeck with the thought that it might work as a novel; there were no strings attached, said Street— he'd settle for life as a lawyer now.

The play had been titled *The Green Lady* and was set in the rugged country of Mendocino. Street had visited there the summers of 1924 and 1925. Then, as now, it was not only beautiful, but an outpost of interesting individuals living on their own idiosyncratic terms, close to nature. The theme of the play involved pantheism and a destructive, obsessive love of nature on the part of the protagonist. In an interview, Street said he tried to dramatize the idea that "when men become hedonists, the very thing they're looking for destroys them." (Interestingly enough, *Cup of Gold* has a similar theme.)

Steinbeck, of course, had spent many long hours talking over the play with Street and had once even made a trip up to Mendocino with him to see it for himself. Some of the technical problems of the play, such as having a forest fire as its central event, could obviously be worked out better in a novel, and the love of nature and forest appealed to Steinbeck, the solitary walker. On the other hand, there was a subtheme that smacked of incest and a general problem of making an obsession believable.

Steinbeck spent the autumn wrestling with the various problems the play presented without solving them. He also wrestled with the problem of commitment that his feelings for Carol presented him, and at least found a solution there – he moved to San Francisco.

Carl Wilhelmson, his friend from Stanford days, was also working hard on his second novel, and the two became roommates. Wilhelmson was even more disciplined than Steinbeck, and his work was being published, so he was a good all-around influence on Steinbeck, or at least as good a one as possible with a young man in love.

Christmas of 1928 was the best Steinbeck had had in years, and a few weeks later he got quite a present – Ted Miller cabled that *Cup of Gold* had been accepted for publication.

Writer's lives abound in ironies; among Steinbeck's was the fact that the publisher was to be none other than Robert McBride & Company, where he had suffered his first miserable defeat a few years before. Seven other publishers had turned down the book, Miller said, and the advance was low – four hundred dollars – but publication and the attention it would bring were probably worth it. Steinbeck agreed and accepted the contract.

McBride was struggling, as were so many businesses as the economy gathered enough negative mass to eventually collapse itself into the Depression later that year. There would be very little money spent to promote the book and no guarantee that all copies printed and bound would be shipped to bookstores. With McBride, Steinbeck's professional career was beginning by leaning on a slender reed indeed. It was enough, however, for he and Carol to become engaged and to set him to work even harder on the novel he was now calling *To the Unknown God*.

That August *Cup of Gold* was published. Steinbeck's disappointment began with the dust jacket – the illustration, better suited for a comic book than a novel, was hideous. The letdown was compounded by the fact that it had been drawn by Mahlon Blaine, his old friend from New York; Steinbeck had recommended him, as a way of thanking him for the early support.

Nothing else about its launch went well. As Steinbeck wrote later in a letter to Ted Miller: "A timid half-hearted advertising campaign which aimed at the wrong people by misdescribing the book, slowness, bad taste in jacket and blurb. Reviewers, after reading that it was an adventure story said, quite truly, that it was a hell of a bad adventure story. It was worse than that. It wasn't an adventure story at all."

He was so irritated at the whole thing that he didn't send his parents copies of the book, but they had the local bookstore in Salinas order copies, proud of him and undoubtedly relieved that he'd finally succeeded, at least in publishing a book. The final blow for him came when he heard that bookstores were stocking it in the juvenile sections and that it still wasn't selling. In the end, most copies ended up on the remainder tables. His consolations were that he'd collected the entire advance and that Carol could hold her head up around her respectable friends who'd wondered what she saw in the impoverished, dour scribbler.

Did *Cup of Gold* deserve its fate? Not really, although were it not for Steinbeck's later success, it certainly wouldn't be in print today.

Briefly, the novel recounts the story of Henry Morgan, who runs away from Wales as an adolescent, his head full of dreams of becoming a buccaneer, only to be sold into indentured servitude in the West Indies. He works for a well-educated and wealthy but ineffectual planter and reads his way avidly through his master's library during this time. His boldness, imagination, and single-mindedness make him a very successful pirate, and his ruthlessness gets him to the top of his profession in short order. He sets out to sack Panama, the richest prize of the New World, partly to cement his reputation but mostly because it harbors the most beautiful and desirable woman in the world, La Santa Rosa (who began it all as "The Lady in Infra-Red" so many years before). Their encounter late in the novel and her scorn for him as a boorish, unheroic babbler reduce his dreams to rubble and his life to a mockery. He betrays his band of pirates for a knighthood and the governorship of Jamaica, eventually dying in bed as a bitterly sad and lonely man.

THE FAILURE OF HIS FIRST BOOK WAS COMPOUNDED BY
ITS HIDEOUS COVER.

If that were all there were to the novel, we could easily say
that *Cup of Gold* deserved its comic-book-illustration cover and
simple-minded publisher's blurb; but Steinbeck had much more in
mind, and a fair amount of what he intended was realized in his
prose, although sometimes awkwardly. He tried to signal his intentions with an ironic subtitle—*A Life of Sir Henry Morgan,*

Buccaneer, with Occasional References to History – and he inserted (sometimes even shoehorned) ironies throughout the incidents of the story.

Steinbeck later wrote to a friend that the principal benefit of the book for him was to purge from himself "all the wise cracks (known by sophomores as epigrams) and all the autobiographical material (which hounds us until we get it said) . . ." Indeed, he never really dealt with his own desires and strivings again.

Not that there are overt similarities between Morgan and Steinbeck, at least for the casual reader. But Morgan's rise, ambitions, single-mindedness, self-doubts, family, and humiliations are all those of the author. Even the final letdown after enormous success is prophesied, with grotesque irony.

Whatever his flaws as a writer and as a man, Steinbeck understood himself and always took responsibility for his actions and his work. *Cup of Gold* is a singular warning that, like Morgan, his ambition and determination are implacable and ineluctable, no matter what the consequences. He will, like the buccaneer, "test his dreams."

Slightly masked by the historical trappings, his parents also appear, and their portraits are interesting. Henry's father is a mediocrity, afraid to dream: "My youth went out of me sticking to coins . . .whereas he [Henry] runs around sticking his finger into pot after pot of cold porridge, grandly confident that each one will turn out to be the porridge of his dreaming. I may not open any kettle, for I believe all porridge to be cold." His mother fares no less well, being pictured as unimaginative and somewhat shrewish: "Oh, the thousand things she chained to Limbo with her incredulity! For many years she had beaten Robert's wild thoughts with a heavy phalanx of common sense; her troop simply charged in and overwhelmed him."

In another passage, he aims a dart at his mother and perhaps other women he had met and cared for: "Every man, so she said, owed it to something or other – his family or his community or himself, I forget just what – to make a success of himself. She was vague as to the nature of success, but she made it very plain that song was not a structure of success."

There are also a number of hints of the writer to come in the careful, sometimes overelaborate use of language, the close observation of nature and animals (and animal metaphors), a slyly dead-pan vein of humor, and a willingness to confront the truths of his characters, however awkward or negative. His dim view of women shows up throughout, also.

In the end, though, the principal undermining factor in the novel is that its theme and, consequently, all the events portrayed in it, rest heavily on irony, which is almost invariably too fragile a foundation for the best work.

Whatever the virtues or drawbacks of his art at this point, the matter was rendered moot by the fact that the handful of reviews the novel got were tepid, and hardly anyone read "this Morgan thing." It sank almost without a trace, and it would be a while before anyone had a chance to evaluate Steinbeck's work again.

6
WHAT'S UP, DOC?

CUP OF GOLD BROUGHT
Steinbeck a measure of financial security, not from his publisher, but
from his father; John Ernst, able to hold the proof of his son's ambition and ability in his two hands in the form of a real book, agreed to
provide John with an allowance of twenty-five dollars a month. The
timing was a bit more than providential—the stock market had
crashed, and the shock waves from it were rapidly heading
westward.

John had moved back to the family cottage in Pacific Grove,
partly to save dwindling money, and Carol moved back in with her
family in San Jose. Other than a camping trip together near Half
Moon Bay for two weeks (during which he spent his days filling
another ledger with the new novel), he and she had not been
together as closely as in the beginning, but at the end of 1929 they
moved to southern California and began living together, first with
Duke Sheffield and then in a cottage nearby.

They settled in Eagle Rock, near Occidental College, where
Sheffield was teaching; Steinbeck may have hoped to get a job there
too. At any rate, the climate was better than up north, and he and
Carol were out from under their families.

They fixed up a rundown house – Steinbeck was an inveterate fixer-upper, happy with tools and manual work – and settled into a routine: he writing, she typing, he rewriting. They acquired the first of many dogs over the years, which Carol walked in her bathing suit, scandalizing the neighborhood. And they got married, on January 14, 1930, in a judge's chambers in Glendale. According to Duke Sheffield, they had a heavy case of the jitters and argued all the way home from the wedding.

The rent on the small house was fifteen dollars a month, and much of their diet was hamburger and stolen avocados from the nearby groves, but by all accounts they were happy. Steinbeck was in a fever of work, rewriting *To an Unknown God* by day and writing a new novel, called *Dissonant Symphony*, at night. Their neighborhood was wooded (which provided free firewood) and sparsely populated, providing him the isolation he preferred.

That spring, Steinbeck mailed the manuscript of "this God thing" to Ted Miller in New York, to be offered to McBride & Company, which had an option on the right of first refusal, and which was not long in coming. Steinbeck professed relief, still unforgiving about the mishandling of his earlier novel, and Miller began shopping the manuscript around. A few months later, not wanting to burden his friend with another task, Steinbeck sent the manuscript of the completed *Dissonant Symphony* to a story contest being run by Charles Scribner's Sons, the publishers of Hemingway, Fitzgerald, and Wolfe. (It is fascinating to wonder what might have happened had he attracted the attention of their great editor, Maxwell Perkins.) He received no reply for quite a long time; the only response he got about his work were the notes from Ted Miller, adding to the roll of publishers who had reacted negatively to "the God thing."

That summer, the house in which he and Carol were living was sold out from under them, and they decided to move back to a familiar setting – the family cottage in Pacific Grove. In letters to friends, Steinbeck was almost jaunty; to Ted Miller, he wrote: "Aren't you getting sick of trundling this white elephant around? It is discouraging, isn't it? Nobody seems to want my work. That doesn't injure me but it must be having a definite effect on you that you are handling a dud." To Carl Wilhelmson, he wrote: "The raps of the last couple of years, i.e. the failure of the Cup, and the failure of my other things to make any impression, seem to have no effect on my spirit whatever . . . Eventually I shall be so good that I cannot be ignored. These years are disciplinary for me."

An even more salutary event that year – disciplinary, emotionally and artistically – was his meeting with Ed Ricketts. Their subsequent friendship provided Steinbeck with a framework and focus for his ideas, as Ricketts became a sounding board, teacher, confessor, partner, and source of philosophy and even characters in Steinbeck's work for the next twenty-five years.

Ricketts is one of the more fascinating characters to pop up in and around modern literature. He was born in Chicago in 1897, which made him five years older than Steinbeck. He attended Illinois State University at Normal for a year, spent time working as an accountant in Texas and a surveyor in New Mexico, then served in the Army before returning home to study at the University of Chicago, which he attended from 1919 to 1922. He attended classes sporadically, like Steinbeck, and he also did not receive a degree, but was and remained exceedingly well read.

In 1923 Ricketts moved to California with A.E. Galigher, his college roommate, and opened Pacific Biologicals, a laboratory and supply house for marine specimens on the edge of Pacific Grove, not far from Cannery Row, and he remained there for the rest of his life. He was married several times, knew many women, and ran a convivial sort of open house at the lab, but was considered basically a loner. He was known as a prodigious consumer of wine and beer, but also as a hard and conscientious worker (all the more notable since he was self-employed). He was affectionately known by the denizens of Cannery Row as "Doc," and he appeared under that name in several Steinbeck novels.

He read endlessly in scientific texts, but his home library also contained a great deal of poetry, and he had done some writing, mostly essays, of which little had yet been published. Within the group of Bohemians in the Monterey–Pacific Grove–Carmel area, he was close to the center, the desired guest and source of approval for many; the lab was the gathering place, the clubhouse. When Steinbeck joined the circle, a number of its members saw him as an obstreperous supporting player stealing scenes from Ricketts, the star of the show. Some of the bitterness and jealousies lasted for many years afterward, and helped to confuse the nature of their relationship.

In fact, each was the friend the other needed. For Steinbeck, here was another man living the life he wanted without regard for convention, guided by his own inner needs, who wouldn't fall by the bourgeois wayside, as many of his other friends and literary acquaintances had. Ricketts liked to drink, and that was important, and he loved thinking and talking and poetry and good writing of all sorts. He was a skeptic who loved to play devil's advocate and had a wry, sometimes caustic sense of humor. All this fitted Steinbeck's own personality neatly. He also became, most importantly, the skeptical reader Steinbeck kept in mind as he wrote.

Ricketts also had an intriguing world view, based partly on his studies with W.C. Allee at the University of Chicago. Allee evolved theories of social behavior among animals that profoundly inspired a generation of students and, through Ricketts, deeply affected Steinbeck's work. Ricketts had also studied and thought about Oriental philosophy, particularly Taoism ("Study the natural order of things and work with it rather than against it, for to try to change what is only sets up resistance . . . In clarity of a still and open mind, truth will be reflected.")

For Ricketts, many of the same criteria obtained, but in Steinbeck he found a friend who could understand much of what he was thinking about, whatever it was at any given moment – which was liable to be anything. In separate interviews some years ago, both Toby Street and an anonymous hooker from Cannery Row recalled that Ricketts liked to explain about marine biology in simple and entertaining ways; in Steinbeck, he had an audience who could keep up with the conversation and even contribute. Time spent collecting specimens in the tide pools around Monterey Bay and talking about their myriad interests was deeply satisfying to both.

It was about the only bright spot in Steinbeck's life at that point. While Carol worked as a secretary for the Monterey Chamber of Commerce, he toiled away on another novel, which he gave up on after a few weeks, fiddled with some short-story ideas, and brooded about the continuing rejections of his work.

In extremis, he banged out a murder mystery, a rank potboiler called *Murder at Full Moon,* in nine days flat. He mailed it to Ted

FRIEND, INSPIRATION, SOURCE, AND MENTOR —
ED RICKETTS IN A QUIET MOMENT.

John Steinbeck

Miller with an apology: "It is quite obvious that people do not want to buy the things I have been writing. Therefore, to make the money I need, I must write the things they want to read. In other words, I must sacrifice artistic integrity for a little while to personal integrity. Remember that when this manuscript makes you sick. And remember that it makes me a great deal sicker that it does you." In case it was published, he chose a pseudonym, Peter Pym. That Christmas, he and Carol were too broke to send out cards.

Of course, the rest of the country was in bad shape, too. The Steinbecks at least had the good fortune to be living by the ocean, and John supplemented their diet by catching fish. Steinbeck later treasured the irony of Edith Mirrielees' advice that he go to Europe, where poverty wasn't a shame, when he recalled that the problem had been settled by the Depression. Friends dropped by with bread, cheese, beans, and plenty of red wine, and, for all the Bohemians, feasts they were. Toby Street recalled that there was "somewhat of a homogeneous flavor" to the crowd as well as their diet.

The Steinbecks didn't invite anyone; friends just showed up— it was an open house. Carol liked having people around, but Street recalls that it was something of a hardship for John, who made up the writing time late at night after the convivial company had left. (Years later, Steinbeck took flying lessons briefly and compared the quiet of the upper air to the peacefulness of a house after a party is over and the solitary host contentedly tidies up.) Ed Ricketts, known as "the Mandarin" because of his way of listening and nodding and tersely commenting with great sagacity, was a visitor, but frequently slipped quietly away to work on a project at the lab; the talk had to be good to hold him.

With three novels adrift on a sea of rejections, Steinbeck felt he had to take another step, advance somehow. He was not a man who asked for help easily, but when Carl Wilhelmson offered to put in a word with his agents in New York, Steinbeck seized the chance. He had just written to Ted Miller, "Financially I should be dead long ago, but I'm not. Things go on and I am not in jail." Shortly afterward: "Wouldn't it be a load off your shoulders if you put the whole caboodle with an agent? I wouldn't mind. It must be rather disheartening to you to collect my rejection slips."

The agents were Mavis McIntosh and Elizabeth Otis. Ted Miller immediately delivered to them the manuscripts of *To an Unknown God* and *Murder at Full Moon,* undoubtedly with a sigh of relief. Later in the year, *Dissonant Symphony* was returned by Scribner's, and it was added to the rotation, along with a batch of short stories.

The murder story never was published; even pulp magazines turned it down, probably to Steinbeck's relief. He withdrew *Dissonant Symphony* after a while when he reread it and decided it just didn't work. However, it had given him an idea for a workable format for a new book; it had been conceived as a series of stories told from the points of view of different people about a man who was never directly seen by the reader—an off-stage protagonist, as it were. Now he began work on a series of interrelated short stories, to be called *The Pastures of Heaven.*

Just south of Salinas, on the way to Monterey, lies Corral de Tierra, a lovely small valley enclosed and hidden by hillsides and startling stone cliffs and spires; it is a classically eclectic California landscape, encompassing cactus, palm trees, and evergreen shrubs and oaks, though the greens of a golf course have replaced the grazing pastures. This is where Steinbeck's Aunt Molly had lived, and he knew every inch of its terrain and many of the stories of its inhabitants. One family had seemed cursed—not malicious in themselves, but the cause of mysterious injury to everyone with whom they came in contact. Steinbeck made this family the connecting device, the common thread and dynamic source of conflict and resolution in the stories.

The influence of Ricketts shows up here, too. The people of the "happy valley" form a colony, interactive, and are observed as objectively as any marine biologist observes the denizens of a tide pool, or any Taoist the workings of nature: no need for judgment; this is just the way it is.

Mavis McIntosh had seen as a major virtue of Steinbeck's work an ability to capture some realistic and interesting aspects of life in California, and she had been urging him to bring that side of his talents forward. He thought *The Pastures of Heaven* fit the bill and worked hard on it during the rest of 1931, completing it in December. The first publisher to read it rejected it. He then had four book manuscripts circulating among editors. "It is a nice thing to know that so many people are reading my books," he joked in a letter to Duke Sheffield. "That is one way of getting an audience."

On February 27, 1932, his thirtieth birthday, he received a wire from Mavis McIntosh informing him that *The Pastures of Heaven* had been accepted by a publisher.

7
THE HOME PLACE

DURING THIS TIME, CAROL
had made an attempt to get out from behind John's pale shadow by opening an advertising agency in partnership with another woman. Monterey's canneries were booming and the Army base at nearby Fort Ord was expanding, so the area was somewhat insulated from the worst effects of the Depression. After an initial early success, however, the agency floundered, and Carol was back at home typing manuscripts again. The Steinbecks were more broke than ever and bought a chess set on a charge account to while away the evenings; they even sold two ducks they'd had as backyard pets, to buy writing paper.

At the beginning of 1932, Carol got a job as secretary to Ed Ricketts for fifty dollars a month, which pleased her greatly—there was never a dull moment around him and the lab. After completing *The Pastures of Heaven*, Steinbeck had gone to work immediately on a rewrite of *To an Unknown God*, which he had originally sworn never to do, after all the drafts he'd written.

The complaints from various editors, and Mavis McIntosh, had centered on the overwrought allegorical and ironic aspects of the plot, which rendered the circumstances and characters unbeliev-

---

able. But as he began his rewrite, a natural event occurred that the storyteller in Steinbeck reacted to galvanically; he felt that it could serve as the realistic yet dramatic underpinning to his muddled novel.

The countryside nearby—indeed, it happens around much of the state of California—had been going through a drought for about ten years. Droughts are insidious, creeping up on you before you know they're there and lingering, destroying things by slow degrees, redefining bleakness under clear and damnably beautiful blue skies; illness and crime increase, and people get touchy and nervous. In December of 1931, the drought broke in a two-week downpour, and people danced in the muddy streets with a crazy joy. Steinbeck reworked his novel into a framework of the greening, the lingering death, and the renewal of the land that gave his characters a better backdrop against which to play out their various fates, while also hewing to the track he'd laid down in *The Pastures of Heaven,* explaining aspects of California life. This effort took him all year.

Meanwhile, the progress toward publication of *The Pastures of Heaven* proved to be torturous. Robert O. Ballou, formerly literary editor of the *Chicago Daily News,* had joined the firm of Cape & Smith sometime before and had helped it become a distinguished firm, but in the troubled climate of 1932, finances were bad and the company had to undergo a reorganization, becoming Jonathan Cape and Robert Ballou, Inc. This delayed the contract and also meant that Steinbeck didn't collect an advance for much of the year. Sometime after the contract was signed, the firm went bankrupt, which meant the contract was invalidated. Ballou then joined the publishing firm of Brewer, Warren and Putnam, and a new contract was issued. Late in 1932, Steinbeck finally got some money for his work, and the book was published. Like his first, it sank pretty much without a trace almost immediately. (The one bright spot for Steinbeck was that his contract guaranteed the publication of his next two books—assuming, of course, that Ballou stayed in business.)

The Pastures of Heaven didn't deserve its sad fate; it is one of Steinbeck's most accessible works. Some of the stories are quite powerful, and together they fulfill his aim of telling what life can be like in the rural valleys of California. The reader is not beaten about the head with ironies, and his observations of nature, work, and ranch life are vivid and shrewd. The multitude of allegories throughout are muted and not intrusive, and the cursed family that is woven through the story can also be seen as simply bourgeois meddlers. In other words, perhaps despite the author's intentions, the book works on a realistic level, while subtly invoking the strength of myth and larger themes than the lives of its characters embody on the surface.

With winter coming on, the Steinbecks moved down to southern California again, settling in the town of Montrose, near Laguna Beach, where John put the finishing touches on the novel finally titled *To a God Unknown*. Their situation was eased somewhat by a small check for the British publication of *The Pastures of Heaven*; the book did a little better there, but not much.

At this point Steinbeck had been plugging away full-time for eight years; he had essentially taught himself to write and to rewrite and never seriously voiced any thought of giving up. His publisher asked for a biography and photograph, both of which might have helped sell his book, and he graciously but firmly turned him down – the books would have to stand on their own. He wrote to Robert Ballou about *To a God Unknown:* "I hope you will like it. The book was hellish hard to write. . . It will probably be a hard book to sell. Its characters are not 'home folks.' They make no more attempt at being sincerely human than the people in the Iliad." Later in the same letter he wrote, "We are very happy. . . Apparently we are heading for the rocks. The light company is going to turn off the power in a few days, but we don't care much. The rent is up pretty soon and then we shall have to move. I don't know where. It doesn't matter. My wife says she would rather go out and meet disaster, than have it sneak up on her. The attacking force has the advantage. I feel the same way. We'll get in the car and drive until we can't buy gasoline any more. Have two more books almost ready to start . . ."

The heavy hand of fate intervened, however. Early in 1933, Steinbeck's mother, then seventy, was hospitalized with high blood pressure and arteriosclerosis, followed by a stroke that left her partly paralyzed. His sisters had settled lives elsewhere, and Steinbeck owed his parents a large debt of gratitude, at the very least; so he and Carol went to Salinas to do what they could for them.

Steinbeck's ambivalence about his parents was troublesome to him. They embodied the bourgeois values he rebelled against and satirized all his life; his father's complaisance and lack of imagination and drive had disappointed him, and his mother's insistence on appearances and respectability and religion had exasperated him. He put distance between them as often and for as long as possible; yet they provided a roof over his head and an allowance that enabled him to keep going, though barely. (Years later, Steinbeck was deeply touched to find that his father had pestered the local bookstore to stock up on his early novels, even though they didn't sell.) Now, his mother was paralyzed and senile, and his father, shattered, could not be told that they were holding a deathwatch.

As single-minded as ever, Steinbeck continued to write. Being back in Salinas, finally confronting his past, had channeled his thinking into his own early life, and he worked on a story about a boy and his pony, helped along by his father's reminiscences as they chatted in the evenings. He wrote to a friend: "It is more being written for discipline than for any other reason. I mean if I can write any kind of a story at a time like this, then I can write stories."

Steinbeck was somewhat cheered during that time by receiving the proofs of *To a God Unknown,* scheduled for publication that autumn. Robert Ballou had begun his own publishing house, and Steinbeck had stayed with him out of loyalty, though Ballou was scrambling for money and Steinbeck's agents had been looking for a more solvent publisher in case he folded.

As usual, Carol pitched in to the task at hand, and she nearly suffered a nervous breakdown helping care for Olive. John Ernst rapidly declined: "He is like an engine that isn't moored tightly and that just shakes itself to pieces," Steinbeck wrote to Duke Sheffield. He had begun a work about the *paisanos* of Monterey, but stalled: "I thought I was going to slip it through, but dad's decline beat me. This is indeed writing under difficulty. The house in Salinas is pretty haunted now . . . This last book is a very jolly one about Monterey *paisanos*. Its tone, I guess, is direct rebellion against all the sorrows of our house. Dad doesn't like characters to swear. But if I had taken all the writing instructions I'd been given, I would be insane . . as long as we can eat and write more books, that's really all I require."

JOHN STEINBECK, SR. SUPPORTED HIS SON STAUNCHLY
WITHOUT REALLY UNDERSTANDING HIM.

John Steinbeck

To a God Unknown came out in November of 1933, just about the last gasp of Robert Ballou, Inc. Only 598 copies were bound and shipped to bookstores. Steinbeck made almost as little money from it as he made from the publication of the first two episodes of *The Red Pony* in *North American Review* magazine that November and December.

In *To a God Unknown* Steinbeck made the first use of his own family as the fabric of his fiction. His hero, Joseph Wayne, is a synthesis of his grandfathers, who came to California to make their fortunes, and Joseph's early life there is based on Steinbeck's childhood observations of ranch life and stories he heard.

Joseph's brothers, who follow him to California after the death of their father, are based more on the Bible and Frazier's *The Golden Bough,* of which Steinbeck had been an avid reader; in fact, the story could have been titled "Joseph and His Brethren." One brother is a romantic wastrel, killed by a rightly jealous husband; another understands animals better than humans and communicates with them in a mystical way; a third is filled with a burning passion for fundamental Christianity and eventually leaves for the pure life of a religious colony in Pacific Grove. It is he, disturbed by Joseph's worship of nature, who kills the oak tree that Joseph feels embodies the spirit of their father and perhaps life itself, and brings on the drought, which Joseph ends by literally sacrificing himself, bleeding to death as the rain finally begins.

If plot were all, *To a God Unknown* would be merely a curiosity, but it contains much of Steinbeck's finest writing on nature – the sheer physical beauty of landscape painted in words is as well realized as anywhere in literature, and the cycles of the earth are painfully acute. In addition, most of the characters and their conflicts have resonances that are good and true and deeply felt, drawn well from the mythic foundations Steinbeck built on. Only the story in which the characters are forced to live falters, and often they overcome it anyway, though not often enough.

During his mother's illness, his father had become so distracted that Steinbeck had to help out in the office. To Carl Wilhelmson he wrote: "Isn't it funny, my two pet horrors, incapacity and ledgers and they both hit at once. I write columns of figures in big ledgers and after about three hours of it I am so stupified that I can't get down to my own work."

His mother died of a final stroke in February 1934. Then the deathwatch began for his father: he wrote Robert Ballou: "Death I can stand but not this slow torture wherein a good and strong man tears off little shreds of himself and throws them away." He, too, had arteriosclerosis, but mainly seemed not to want to live.

The *paisano* stories Steinbeck had worked into *Tortilla Flat* that year had begun with jottings two years before, enriched by trips to various low-life bars with Ed Ricketts, who moved easily in all circles. Susan Gregory, an acquaintance who taught at Monterey's high school, was also a poet and a descendant of generations of Californians, and she passed along many stories of local life; a friend of hers, Harriet Gragg, whose father had settled in California in 1837, was also a source. Although the high jinks of the *paisanos* had indeed been good therapy for Steinbeck, the book had by now what had become the usual difficulties finding a publisher.

Around this time, his conversations with Ricketts and his readings on biology and other sciences coalesced into a theory on the actions of men in groups, which he first called the "group-man" theory and later "phalanx," from the Greek battle formations of tightly massed troups. It provided Steinbeck with a fictional symbolism he felt was tremendously important. He wrote to Duke Sheffield: "The fascinating thing to me is the way the group has a soul, a drive, an intent, an end, a method, a reaction and a set of tropisms which in no way resembles the same things possessed by the men who make up the group. These groups have always been considered as individuals multiplied. And they are not so. They are beings in themselves, entities."

In a batch of letters written that year to various friends, Steinbeck expounded on the theory and even refined it as he wrote them. Back in Pacific Grove after his mother's death, he spent many hours with Ricketts, developing "the argument of phalanx."

In the meantime, however, he was suddenly faced with something new for him—literary acceptance. *The Red Pony* had proven popular, and the editors of *North American Review* wanted more stories, which he sent; three more were published that year, 1934, and one was awarded the O. Henry prize as one of the best short stories of the year. He savored the irony that he'd reached more readers in one issue of the magazine than with his three novels.

The fourth, *Tortilla Flat,* was having rough sledding. Robert Ballou didn't much care for it and, in severe financial trouble, declined to pick up his option to publish it; other publishers had the same opinion.

But Steinbeck, all unknowing, had a champion. Ben Abramson, a bookseller in Chicago, had read the stories and then ordered copies of the available novels (*To a God Unknown* and *The Pastures of Heaven*—*Cup of Gold* was out of print), which he also liked and talked customers into buying. Abramson was visited one day by Pascal "Pat" Covici, a partner in the prestigious house of Covici-Friede in New York, and he talked Covici into a copy of *The Pastures of Heaven,* which the publisher read on the train back to New York. Covici immediately contacted McIntosh and Otis, found that Steinbeck was free of obligations to other publishers, and made an offer not only to publish *Tortilla Flat,* but to reissue the earlier novels. His company was struggling and there would be no large advances, but the two men took to each other immediately in their correspondence, and their personal and professional relationship lasted all their lives. Steinbeck had at last found the publisher he needed, a man with as much fortitude and imagination as himself.

Both would be necessary for the work in which Steinbeck was then immersed—a tough novel about a murderous strike.

8

A BATTLE AND A BAN

As painful as it had been

for Steinbeck to return and live in Salinas, the experience had been good for him; he had been running away from it and his family for years, denying himself a large part of his experience. By reclaiming some of it with *The Pastures of Heaven,* he had at last found his voice, and the short stories published in 1934 had confirmed this. Now, in his work, allegories were underpinnings that strengthened plot and character instead of determining and distorting them, and his early work experiences and observations could prove useful.

Even fifty years ago, the differences between Salinas and the Monterey area were pronounced (though not as much as today); less than twenty miles apart, they might as well be in two different states. Salinas today retains its agricultural base and middle-class small-town life, and Steinbeck would still be out of place there.

In the mid-thirties, Salinas was in a tumult of labor unrest, as were many other agricultural areas in the state. Labor was getting organized, and so were the landowners and farmers. The Communist Party was especially active, seeing in the systematic abuse of migrant workers a golden opportunity for power. Strikes were met with brutal vigilante repression and editorial hysteria; bloodshed was all too common.

Steinbeck's natural inclinations would have been to side with the oppressed anyway, but having worked in the fields gave him an especially acute view of the problems. On the other hand, he had no tolerance for the Communists, whom he felt were willing to manipulate people and even incite violence in order to achieve their political ends.

Sometime during 1934, Steinbeck had met a Communist organizer who was on the run, hiding out in Salinas until whatever situation he'd provoked had cooled down. Steinbeck had smuggled the man some food and spent many hours in conversation with him, out of which came his short story "The Raid," which was published by *North American Review.* He thought of writing a novel that would be the biography of a Communist, then tried converting the story into a journalistic account of a strike; but it wouldn't be contained so neatly. In a letter, he wrote: "I'm not interested in strike as means of raising men's wages, and I'm not interested in ranting about justice and oppression, mere outcroppings which indicate the condition. But man hates something in himself. He has been able to defeat every natural obstacle, but himself he cannot win over unless he kills every individual. And this self-hate which goes so closely in hand with self-love is what I wrote about. The book is brutal. I wanted to be merely a recording consciousness, judging nothing, simply putting down the thing. I think it has the thrust, almost crazy, that mobs have. It is written in disorder."

He called the book *In Dubious Battle,* from a passage in Milton's *Paradise Lost* that summed up his own struggle and philosophy:

> *Innumerable force of Spirits armed,*
> *That durst dislike his reign, and, me preferring,*
> *His utmost power with adverse power opposed*
> *In Dubious Battle on the plains of Heaven,*
> *And shook His throne. What though the field be lost?*
> *All is not lost—the unconquerable will,*
> *And study of revenge, immortal hate,*
> *And courage never to submit or yield:*
> *And what is else not to be overcome?*

Steinbeck finished the book early in 1935 and for the first time in his career did not immediately begin writing another one. He was exhausted right down to the bone, as was Carol, who had a full-time job with the State Emergency Relief Administration and spent her nights typing the thousands of words her husband produced every day. They had no way of knowing that their ordeal was about to end.

Steinbeck was so skeptical about his prospects, even with *Tortilla Flat* about to be published, that he applied for the James Phelan Award for Literature, which was a grant of a thousand dollars—enough for he and Carol to live on for two years, he reckoned. Despite his circumstances, he maintained his jaunty humor in a letter to Ann Hadden, librarian of the Palo Alto Public Library, whom he asked to sponsor him:

I have all the vices in a very mild way except that of narcotics, unless coffee and tobacco are classed as narcotics. I have been in jail once for a night a long time ago, a result of a combination of circumstance, exuberance and a reasonable opinion that I could lick a policeman. The last turned to to be undemonstrable. I don't think the trustees would be interested, but they might. I am married and quarrel violently with my wife and we both enjoy it very much. And last, I am capable of a tremendous amount of work. I have just finished a novel of a hundred and twenty thousand words, three drafts in a little over four months. I am embarrassed for having to ask any one to vouch for me. I seems it would be better if I could simply submit a book and be judged upon the strength of it.

In that he may have been correct; he did not receive the award.

PASCAL COVICI WAS THE

first publisher Steinbeck had who made an effort in producing a book; he commissioned Ruth Gannett to illustrate *Tortilla Flat* with whimsical drawings and had the book designed with care. He also coordinated an effective prepublication publicity campaign that built up interest in the book and its author. Many of the initial reviews were good, including one by influential critic Lewis Gannett, husband of the illustrator, and the book was a success from the start.

Steinbeck's father died a week before the publication of *Tortilla Flat* in May of 1935. They had grown closer, and Steinbeck felt bereft, yet relieved that his father's ordeal was over. "Poor silent man all his life," Steinbeck wrote to Elizabeth Bailey, his godmother. "I feel very badly, not about his death, but about his life, for he told me only a few months ago that he had never done anything he wanted to do. Worst of all he hadn't done the work he wanted to do."

Also worrisome to him that spring was the report that Covici was hesitant to publish *In Dubious Battle*. One of his editors had written a long and damning report on the novel, questioning Stein-beck's grasp of Communist ideology on the one hand, and then say-ing that the book would undoubtedly be fiercely attacked by both the left and the right. Steinbeck was deeply angered: "My informa-tion for this book came mostly from Irish and Italian communists whose training was in the field, not in the drawing room . . . And if attack has ever hurt the sale of a book I have yet to hear of it."

Covici was somewhat hoist with his own petard; his publicity campaign for *Tortilla Flat* had worked well, and other publishers were curious about this "new" author. In March another of Stein-beck's stories was published, and the *O. Henry Prize Stories of 1934,* containing one of his, was coming out. Under the prodding of Elizabeth Otis, who thereafter handled all of Steinbeck's work at the agency, Covici relented. He even made a trip to California in order to meet Steinbeck for the first time and personally present him with his first royalty check, the princely sum of $299.44, and assurances that there would be more to come.

Among the people who were not amused by *Tortilla Flat*'s grow-ing popularity was the Monterey Chamber of Commerce. Steinbeck gleefully reported that local hotel clerks were being instructed to tell guests who inquired that there was no such place.

Steinbeck maintained a distance between him and his new suc-cess. "Curious that this second-rate book, written for relaxation, should cause this fuss," he wrote to Elizabeth Otis, adding, "In your dealings you need make no compromise at all for financial considera-tions as far as we are concerned. Too many people are trapped into promises by gaudy offers . . . we've gone through too damned much trying to keep the work honest and in a state of improvement to let it slip now in consideration of a little miserable popularity. I'm scared to death of popularity. It has ruined everyone I know . . . I suppose it is bad tactics but I am refusing the usual things—the radio talks, the autograph racket, the author's afternoons and the rest of the clut-ter—politely, I hope, but firmly."

FOR MUCH OF HIS LIFE, THE FAMILY COTTAGE IN
PACIFIC GROVE WAS A REFUGE FOR JOHN.

In *Tortilla Flat* Steinbeck held up a fun-house mirror to middle-class respectability and hugely enjoyed the comic distortions he created, but he had quite a kettle of satiric fish to fry, too; his indolent characters' casual but unceasing pursuit of wine, women, and easy money are rationalized in elaborate and charming conversations and schemes that make a mockery of the rituals of conventional society.

The allegorical underpinnings of *Tortilla Flat* are the Arthurian legends Steinbeck loved so much: "For Danny's house was not unlike the Round Table, and Danny's friends were not unlike the knights of it." The chapters are headed with mock-serious sentences: "How Danny, home from the wars, found himself an heir, and how he swore to protect the helpless"; "How Jesus Maria Corcoran, a good man, became an unwilling vehicle of evil." (These were added some time after the manuscript was finished, as a unifying device.)

Like every good legend, *Tortilla Flat* has a hero, Danny, who rises from obscurity, attains a great height, and performs noble deeds, and, through a tragic flaw, suffers a dying fall from grace. Danny is first burdened by property and then creates a unit, his band of friends, in which his individuality is lost by their dependence on him; he dies destroying the unit, and his friends complete the drama by allowing his house to burn down before going their separate ways.

Steinbeck weaves a dense and colorful tapestry in this short book; Danny and the gang have little to do, and so in some episodes are merely observers or listeners. At least two of the stories were written years before—the story of Sweets Ramirez, who "took such gifts as walked by in jeans" and is won by Danny's present of a vacuum cleaner, even though there is no electricity on the Flat, was written originally at Stanford, and the story of the Mexican corporal, who was cuckolded by a captain and who wanted his son to grow up to be a general so he could take the better things of life more easily, had originally been told to him by a fellow laborer. The language, an elaborate rendering of English-spoken-as-Spanish, adds considerably to the charm of the book. Steinbeck had an excellent ear for the rhythms of speech, a virtue that goes too often unnoticed by most critics, but any actor who has played or read his work aloud appreciates the ease with which it can be spoken.

That summer *Tortilla Flat* landed on the best-seller list.

Despite Steinbeck's attempts to retain a measure of privacy and keep himself aloof from the hoopla that can surround a best-seller, he found the attentions coming his way distracting. He was trying to begin a big book, a novel he estimated would take two years to write, embodying his phalanx theory. He had hopes that *In Dubious Battle* might give him an odd respite. He wrote to Elizabeth Otis: "Myths form quickly and I want no tag of humorist on me, nor any other kind. Besides, IDB would reduce popularity to nothing . . ."

In the meantime, he and Carol went to Mexico by automobile for an indefinite stay, the first vacation they had ever taken. They had a good time in Mexico City, but within a month he was ready to return—he couldn't get any work done there, he said.

While there, they received a wire from McIntosh & Otis informing them that the movie rights to *Tortilla Flat* had been sold. The cable was cryptic, and Steinbeck wrote back, "It is rather amusing what the Mexican operator must have thought of your wire – '4000 dollars for Tortilla.' Probably thought it was either a code word or a race horse."

In a longer letter to Elizabeth Otis shortly afterward, he wrote, "Maybe with this security I can write a better book. Maybe not. Certainly though I can take a little longer and write a more careful one. And it will be possible to contemplate an illness without panic. I do not see what even Hollywood can make of Tortilla with its episodic treatment, but let them try and I won't go to their picture so that is all right."

He also had his first (but far from last) banning, by Ireland; it was not amused by *Tortilla Flat*.

The Steinbecks came back to California by way of New York, where he signed the movie contract and finally met the agents who had gone through so much with them. As usual, Steinbeck passed up the opportunity of interviews or any other publicity to hype the forthcoming publication of *In Dubious Battle*.

Back home, just at the end of 1935, Steinbeck was displeased to find that *Tortilla Flat* had won a prestigious award, the Commonwealth Club of California's gold medal for the best novel of the year about California. He refused to go the the awards dinner and wrote a long explanation to Joseph Henry Jackson, book reviewer of the *San Francisco Chronicle,* an early champion of Steinbeck's work and, as a good friend, one of the few people Steinbeck would bother explaining himself to:

Nothing like this has ever happened to me before. The most I have had to dodge has been a literary tea or an invitation from a book shop to lecture and autograph. This is the first and God willing the last prize I shall ever win.

The whole early part of my life was poisoned with egotism, a reverse egotism, of course, beginning with self-consciousness. And then gradually I began to lose it.

In the last few books I have felt a curious richness as though my life had been multiplied through having been identified in a most real way with people who were not me. I have loved that. And I am afraid, terribly afraid, that if the bars ever go down, if I become a trade mark, I shall lose the ability to do that. When I do I shall stop working because it won't be fun any more . . .

This is not clear, concise, objective thinking, but I have never been noted for any of these things. If I were a larger person I would be able to do this and come out of it untouched. But I am not . . . I have no social gifts and practically no social experience . . .

Jackson took care to send the gold medal to Steinbeck, who was enormously amused years later to discover that it was actually gold-plated, and thinly at that.

TWO OTHER NOTEWORTHY

events occurred that year. A friend of the Steinbecks, Peter O'Crotty, had begun a small magazine called the *Monterey Beacon* and had asked Steinbeck for contributions. The author obliged with a story he'd had lying around; it was called "A Snake of One's Own" and tells of a woman who visits a commercial laboratory to buy a rattlesnake — male — only to watch it kill and eat a white rat. It is a powerful and evocative story, based on a real incident, and marks the first appearance in Steinbeck's fiction of Ed Ricketts.

The second was in the nature of a private joke. Steinbeck sent in a batch of poems by "Amnesia Glasscock." They were quite ribald and had to be tidied up a little for publication. It was assumed for years that they were the work of Steinbeck, but recently Carol admitted that she was the author, noting that she was influenced by Dorothy Parker. The Steinbecks thought once of having them published as a book, but nothing came of it. One of the poems, titled "Four Shades of Navy Blue," shows the flavor; in part it reads:

> I sing of the beauty of breeches on sailors
> The pants of the navy, sons of the sea.
> Those round little seats in their snug woolen casings,
> Have rhythm and color and pure symmetry . . .
> That insolent swagger is utterly charming,
> I'm lost in a rapture that's full and complete.
> I say it with frankness that should be disarming,
> There's beauty to me in the pants on the fleet.

(A peril of anonymity — years later a writer, assuming the work to be Steinbeck's, used it as "proof" that he was a secret homosexual. He may have been roused by another of the poems, which ended):

> Our men grow more emasculate
> Through every passing hour,
> For men were men in those dead days,
> And a pansy was a flower.

"The Genius" may have been based on close observation:

A fact it is, and cannot be denied,
An artist's temper is a source of pride.
The fervid groans, the tearing of the hair,
The heaving chest, the posture of despair,
Give evidence of gifts most rare . . .
And it is his inalienable right
To brood upon a sonnet through the night.
For only by these signs can he be known
As one not built of common flesh and bone
But obviously hot-house grown.

John Steinbeck

9

E̲LEVEN-CENT
COTTON,
FORTY-CENT
MEAT

T̲HE YEAR 1936 WAS A YEAR
of tumult for Steinbeck, both in good and bad ways. It opened with a
bang, as *In Dubious Battle* was published to even more controversy
than anyone had foreseen.

A daily review in the *New York Times* called it "an honest book
and an exciting story," and in a longer Sunday review in that paper,
John Chamberlain said, "As a thinker, Mr. Steinbeck may be crazy;
as a dramatic artist, he is as brilliant as he is versatile."

The *Daily Worker,* the official newspaper of the Communist
Party, of course had a different reaction: "To clamp down on Steinbeck because he is still muddled about a number of things with refer-
ence to the class struggle is not the job of a Marxian critic." Its
readers, however, didn't hesitate to take up the cudgels, and the paper's letters column became a battleground of angry rhetoric about
the book.

Opinions in the influential, and mostly liberal, weekly magazines on the East Coast were sharply divided also; one, in *The Nation,* particularly aroused Steinbeck's ire. Mary McCarthy, who
was beginning to make a name for herself, said the novel was "academic, wooden, inert . . . Mr. Steinbeck for all his long and fre-

quently pompous exchanges offers only a few rather childish, often reiterated generalizations . . . He may be a natural story-teller; but he is certainly no philosopher, sociologist, or strike technician."

One reason for Steinbeck's anger was that *Tortilla Flat* had been savaged the year before in *The Nation,* and he believed that that attack had also come from Mary McCarthy. His friend Joseph Henry Jackson had written a commentary in the *San Francisco Chronicle* that referred to that piece as "a patronizing sneer from a reviewer afflicted with the class itch," and Steinbeck believed that McCarthy had been waiting to "ambush" his next book in retaliation. In fact, it was a mixup—the earlier review had been written by Helen Neville, but *The Nation* ran its reviewer's bylines at the end of reviews, and Steinbeck had seen a clipping headed by McCarthy's name, which actually belonged to the preceding review. The feud may seem silly in retrospect, but it's possible that it contributed to the negative view of Steinbeck held by some of McCarthy's Eastern colleagues, which did real harm to his reputation. He never missed an opportunity to knock McCarthy for the rest of his life. And her ex-husband, Edmund Wilson, reciprocated savagely in print at every opportunity.

Broadway producer Herman Shumlin, who had a fondness for sweeping dramas, optioned the book; Clifford Odets' play *Waiting for Lefty* had been a great success the year before, and he may have thought the Broadway stage was ready for an epic strike drama. His choice as the adapter was a curious one—the urbane and sophisticated John O'Hara, a quintessential East Coast dandy well known for his short stories in the *New Yorker.*

On the surface, Steinbeck and O'Hara were wildly unalike, but in fact they had a great deal in common, especially in their attitudes about work and literary critics. O'Hara had been working in the movies in Hollywood, and he came up to the cottage in Pacific Grove for a visit. The two men got along well and became lifelong friends (and even stablemates at *Collier's* magazine years later). O'Hara brought the outside world into the Steinbeck home with his tales of literary life in New York and the movie business of Hollywood; he knew most of the great American writers of his generation, unlike the almost reclusive Steinbeck, but John felt no stirrings of ambition to be part of either, at least not then.

With all the talk of theater between them, Steinbeck thought it only natural to invite Toby Street over to meet O'Hara, and then Ed Ricketts, who was not only a character in *In Dubious Battle,* but another explainer of the phalanx theory that underpinned the events of the book, which theory O'Hara did not seem to have grasped. O'Hara wrote Steinbeck years later: "It is a warm and good friendship that began that warm afternoon in Pacific Grove, A.D. 1936, with some Mexican dish cooking on the stove, an English saddle hanging on a peg, your high school diploma on the wall, and you trying to explain about phalanx man."

The projected dramatization never went through. O'Hara wasn't really comfortable with the characters of the working men, and the novel resisted translation into drama. Steinbeck also tried blocking out some scenes, and said it was "lousy, lifeless." He wasn't too bothered by the experience, however; the friendship with O'Hara was enough of a reward.

ONE OF THE THINGS THAT

had pleased Steinbeck about *In Dubious Battle* was that it was so different from *Tortilla Flat;* all his life, he resisted critical pigeonholing, the idea of becoming a "brand name" who would become the slave of the public's desire for "more of the same" rather than following his own desires. "I want no tag of humorist," he had written after the success of the *paisano* novel, and then added, "nor any other." Late in his career, some of his literary gear-shifting seemed almost capricious and did a great deal to confuse critics and the public alike. He ended up being tagged as versatile, too much so for his own good. For the moment, though, the cold and savage bitterness of *In Dubious Battle* served well to force readers to take Steinbeck seriously and look forward to his future works.

The most important aspect of the novel for Steinbeck was the least so for many critics, even those who liked the book: the phalanx theory, which he had been thinking hard about since 1933, when he wrote to a friend, "Ed Ricketts has dug up all the scientific material and more than I need to establish the physical integrity of the thing . . . Old phalanxes break up in a fine imitation of death of the man unit. New phalanxes are born under proper physical and spiritual conditions. They may be of any size from the passionate three who are necessary to receive the holy spirit, to the race which over-night develops a soul for conquest, to the phalanx which commits suicide through vice or war or disease. When your phalanx needs you it will use you, if you are the material to be used. You will know when the time comes, and when it does come, nothing you can do will let you escape." Whatever the merits of this argument, Stein-beck dramatizes it in a context that is powerfully believable.

In Dubious Battle traces the brief career of Jim Nolan as a labor organizer, from idealistic convert to the Communist Party to useful martyr only a short time later. Although Jim is the book's protago-nist, he is far from a hero; neither are most of the other characters notable in the plot, with the possible exception of Doc Burton (the Ricketts representation). This exchange is typical of the book's tone:

Mac laughed. "I'm surprised at you, Albert. Haven't you got no idears about the nobility of labor?"

"I got nothing," Albert said. "No idears, no money, no nothing."

"Nothing to lose but your chains," Jim put in softly.

"Bull," said Albert, "nothing to lose but my hair."

"You got this truck," Mac said. "How'd we get this stuff back without a truck?"

"This truck's got me," Albert complained. "The God-damned truck's just about two-bitted me to death." He looked sadly ahead. His lips scarcely moved when he talked. "When I'm workin' and I get three dollars to the good and I get set to look me up a floozy, somethin' on this buggy busts and costs three dollars. Never fails. God damn truck's worse 'n a wife."

Jim said earnestly, "In any good system, you'd have a good truck."

"Yeah? In any good system, I'd have a floozy . . ."

Mac is the senior Party man showing Jim the ropes as they try to organize the workers through a strike against apple growers who are brutalizing and exploiting the pickers and their families. Jim, how-ever, is a zealot, a true believer, and he quickly and ruthlessly over-takes his mentor as the driving force:

"I wanted you to use me. You wouldn't because you got to like me too well . . . That was wrong. Then I got hurt. And sitting here waiting, I got to know my power. I'm stronger than you, Mac. I'm stronger than anything in the world, because I'm going in a straight line. You and all the rest have to think of women and tobacco and liquor and keeping warm and fed." His eyes were cold as wet river stones. "I wanted to be used. Now I'll use you, Mac. I'll use myself and you . . .

In the end, killed by a double-barreled shotgun blast in the face, Jim's ghastly corpse serves as a rallying point for the faltering strikers, who had been about to give up in fear of armed vigilantes ("pool-room Americans," Steinbeck called them). Mac, normally a poor orator, is galvanized and seizes the moment, propping up his awful display and crying out, "Comrades! He didn't want nothing for himself—." It's a chilling ending to the book, somewhat reminiscent of Joe Hill's gallows cry: "Don't mourn, boys—organize!"

The strikers are seen throughout as pawns for both sides to manipulate, and the farmers' association is a shadowy, evil force dedicated to making money without caring a bit about the rootless people who follow the harvest and who are exploited by the process. There are a handful of decent people in the book, one an independent farmer who gives the strikers work and allows them to camp on his land, and the other a sympathetic doctor, who sets up sanitary facilities and ministers to the sick in the camp so the strikers can't be run off as a health hazard.

Doc Burton, as noted, is modeled on Ed Ricketts, to a degree that goes beyond the needs of the plot; in fact, he is the least successfully realized character in the book, probably because Steinbeck was attempting to pay tribute to his friend and mentor. Whenever he did so directly, as he did in several later works, he tended to sentimentalize Ricketts; even with his considerable narrative powers, Steinbeck, like everyone else who knew the man, simply couldn't adequately sum him up.

As a kind of Greek chorus commenting on the action and even counterpointing it, Doc Burton is more successful. When Jim, in all his idealism and blind naiveté, says all good things begin in violence, Doc replies, "There aren't any beginnings . . . Nor any ends. It seems to me that man has engaged in a blind and fearful struggle out of a past he can't remember, into a future he can't foresee nor understand. And man has met and defeated every obstacle, every enemy except one. He cannot win over himself."

Interestingly, Doc Burton's philosophy renders him ineffective in the course of the novel's events, so that by the end of the book, when action and resolution are called for, he simply disappears. Mac says, "Doc was a nice guy, but he didn't get anywhere with his high-falutin' ideas. His ideas didn't go anywhere, just in a circle." Although the idea intrigued him, the Way of the Tao was not for Steinbeck, in the end.

Two other aspects of the novel illustrate Steinbeck's growth and mastery of technique. The texture of the prose is deliberately varied; while the speech of the characters is rendered with colorful naturalness, the narrative portions are starkly objective and color-less—even the metaphors are tight and grim. This has a way of teasing his readers, engaging us at times, at other times keeping us stiffly at arm's length; the effect is a series of jolts that keep us alert and fascinated.

The use of Biblical and Christian mythology is subtle but permeates the novel and provides it with much of its power. Jim and Mac and the strikers, rebelling against the established order, have distinct parallels in the "dubious battle" between the forces of God and Satan "on the plains of Heaven" that Milton describes in *Paradise Lost*. There is also a parallel with the expulsion from the Garden of Eden, where mankind exchanged paradise for an immortal soul. Even a reader without much knowledge of Christian mythology can't fail to be touched by the powerful resonances echoing throughout the story. It was an incredibly ambitious attempt for the basically self-taught novelist, a terribly complex load of literary freight to lay on a simple track of plot; but Steinbeck pulled it off, and *In Dubious Battle* remains one of his best books.

THERE WOULD BE NO MORE

privacy and seclusion for Steinbeck—he was a public figure now, like it or not; but he fought hard to keep his life the way he wanted it. He and Carol bought a two-acre lot fifty miles north of Monterey, on the edge of the quiet little town of Los Gatos. Carol supervised the building of the house, in a grove of oaks, manzanita, and madrone trees, and, though their nearest neighbor lived a mile away, John built an eight-foot-high grapestake fence around the property.

Their arrival was noted in the local press, however: "Noted Author to Join Colony Here of Literary Folk" was one chilling headline, and soon curiosity-seekers were wending their way down his gravel road. Steinbeck had, in a moment of whimsy, carved

"Steinbeckia" in his gate, but now he changed the name to "Arroyo del Ajo," which translates as "Garlic Gulch."

While the house was being built, he holed up in Pacific Grove, happy to be working hard on a "new little novel" about a pair of itinerant ranch hands, called for the moment "Something That Happened." He was trying out a new technique and later said it was designed to teach him to write for the theater.

The idea may have come out of his talks with John O'Hara, who tried all his life to write for the theater, without much success. The theater holds a great allure for novelists, being a communal effort instead of a painfully solitary one, and offering a writer a chance to hear cheers and applause. Henry James, Somerset Maugham, Graham Greene, Albert Camus, and many others have been so seduced. Furthermore, for a successful playwright in those days, the money was better. The fact that many playwrights envy the solitude of novelists rarely alters the equation—the grass seems always greener on the other side of the footlights.

Steinbeck finished a draft of the novel quickly, but then his dog, left alone one night, chewed the manuscript to pieces. "I was pretty mad but the poor little fellow may have been acting critically," he wrote to his agent, adding that the punishment had been light, as there was no sense ruining a good dog over a manuscript. He began again, with a new title—*Of Mice and Men,* from the Robert Burns poem about best-laid plans—suggested by Ed Ricketts. The new draft was finished by early summer and was enthusiastically received by his agents and Pat Covici; Annie Laurie Williams, who handled theatrical matters for McIntosh & Otis, thought it would translate easily into a play—exactly Steinbeck's idea. It would be the first book of his to be published smoothly, without dissension or even quibbles.

In the meantime, Steinbeck received his first newspaper assignment, one that would have a profound effect on his life. The furor over *In Dubious Battle* had subsided somewhat, but it had had an effect, helping to call attention to the increasingly horrendous plight of migrant workers in California. George West, chief editorial writer for the *San Francisco News,* commissioned Steinbeck to write a series of articles on the situation, which was called "The Harvest Gypsies." Since it was one of these rare times when he didn't have another book to write immediately, Steinbeck accepted with alacrity.

There had been something of a farm-labor surplus for years before the 1930s, but it became more and more acute as the decade ground on. It began to consist of whole families, dispossessed either by general economic conditions or by being "dusted off" their farms. Growers and their associations encouraged the surplus as a way of "stabilizing" wages — in 1932, some advertised rates were fifteen cents an hour, and in 1933, twelve-and-a-half cents. A song of the time, "A Share-Cropper's Lament," went:

> Eleven-cent cotton and forty-cent meat
> How in the world can a poor man eat?
> Eleven-cent cotton, eight bucks pants
> Who in the world can have a chance?

The migrants were the responsibility of the Rural Rehabilitation program, which attempted to provide them with public health services and otherwise improve their living conditions. Only a few people realized that a major, and probably permanent, population shift was occurring (more than 87,000 migrants entered California in the harvest season of 1935–36) and that something more had to be done about these people than encouraging them to move on when the crops were picked. A proposal was put forth to build a chain of camps to provide decent living conditions for the migrants in the rural areas of the state. The resistance from the agricultural establishment, which thought camps would encourage migrants to settle, was ferocious.

The Rural Rehabilitation program was federal, however, and the state could impede but not stop it; soon after the proposal was accepted, in the spring of 1935, it was made part of the stronger federal Resettlement Administration under Rexford Tugwell, one of Franklin Roosevelt's inner circle. Work was soon begun on the camps.

The first camp was built near Marysville, north of Sacramento, in 1935, and a man named Tom Collins was chosen to run it. Collins was one of those people of whom adventure fiction is made, who turn up in a place, with a mysterious past, take hold of a difficult situation and handle it with nervy vigor and imagination, and then disappear. He not only ran labor camps, but evolved a philosophy and workable systems for them. After the Marysville camp was set up,

---

another was built at Arvin, near Bakersfield, at the lower end of the San Joaquin Valley, and Collins moved there to run it.

One of his jobs was to keep weekly reports on doings at the camp, and he turned them into an odd literary form all his own – the most unlikely reports ever filed by a federal employee. They contain songs and poems and folk wisdom of the migrants, editorials on living conditions, journalistic accounts of life for the workers outside the camps, anecdotes of encounters with hostile growers, and detailed inventories of the origins and possessions of the migrants.

Some of these reports were forwarded by Collins' superior to the *San Francisco News,* where they were excerpted; the *News* was a feisty Scripps-Howard newspaper, and about the only one to take a stand on the plight of the workers. It was only natural that when Steinbeck got his *News* assignment, one of the first people he looked up was Tom Collins.

Most of Steinbeck's best work began with real people and first-hand observation, and in Tom Collins he had the richest imaginable source and best guide. *The Grapes of Wrath,* which eventually came out of their friendship, is dedicated to him.

The camp at Arvin, which Steinbeck visited, was known as "Weedpatch," and appears in the novel as "Wheatpatch." Collins showed Steinbeck around, gave him copies of his reports, and talked long into the night – he was a great talker. He introduced Steinbeck to Sherman Eastom, who was the Camp Committee Chairman (and a migrant), and later Steinbeck met Eastom's son at a nearby squatters' camp; the young man was hiding out from the law, and he became the model for Tom Joad. When Steinbeck returned to the house in Los Gatos, he had an armload of material for his articles and an inspiration. He wrote to a friend, "Down the country I discovered a book like nothing in the world."

As he wrote his articles, the labor situation worsened considerably, and for a little while there was some doubt whether the *News* would print the series. A more typical view held by the media ran in the *Yuba City Herald* under the headline MIGRANT CAMP IS RED HOTBED. "The Federal migrant camp in the city of Marysville is becoming a Red hotbed, a breeding place for the fomenting of strikes to destroy the peach crops of Sutter, Yuba and Butte counties. The U.S. Government is sheltering these Reds at night,

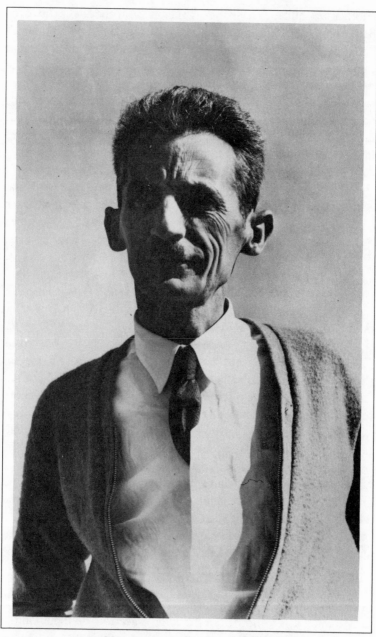

TOM COLLINS WAS STEINBECK'S GUIDE THROUGH
THE HELL OF THE MIGRANT CAMPS.

John Steinbeck

providing them with roofs, beds and living accommodations, together with a willing audience . . . The Marysville City Government can either keep that migrant camp cleared of Reds or the ranchers will level it to the ground."

That this sort of thing was more than mere rhetoric was proven that September, when a lettuce-pickers' strike in Salinas was brutally crushed by an officially appointed paramilitary force of "deputized" vigilantes acting under a local version of martial law. Anything even slightly resembling civil rights for the workers was simply voided, and no higher governments interceded.

Steinbeck may have thought he had made his peace with his former home town, but this breach opened up all the old angers again, and the idea for a new novel curdled rapidly into satire, as exemplified by the title, *L'Affaire Lettuceberg*. His idea was to etch a series of acidulous portraits of the burghers of Salinas, in all their hypocrisy. He worked on the novel that fall, into the winter, and then put it aside when he saw how his anger had contorted his prose.

Tom Collins visited the Steinbecks at Los Gatos several times; Steinbeck had been enchanted by the camp reports and had offered to edit them into a manuscript and to use his influence to get it published as a book. It was an unlikely task for Steinbeck, who was never a particularly good collaborator and who had no particular skills or experience as an editor, and the project finally floated aimlessly, buoyed up by nothing more than good intentions. (It is interesting to speculate what might have happened had it been turned over to Carol, who by then did have some editing skills; one has to wonder if it ever came up.)

Finally, on October 5, 1936, "The Harvest Gypsies" appeared and ran for a week, complete with photographs that documented the stories. The paper gave Steinbeck plenty of space, and the essays are fine work. He began by telling who the migrants were and what they faced:

They arrive in California usually having used up every resource to get here, even to the selling of the poor blankets and utensils and tools on the way to buy gasoline. They arrive bewildered and beaten and usually in a state of semi-starvation, with only one necessity to face immediately, and that is to find work at any wage in order that the family may eat . . . The unique nature of California agriculture requires that these migrants exist, and requires that they move about. [They] are needed, and they are hated. Arriving in a district they find the dislike always meted out by the resident to the foreigner, the outlander.

Steinbeck used his novelist's skill in another section, poignantly relating stories of three families from the top to the bottom of the social scale among migrants—the ones at the bottom were the ones who'd been at it longest, who were malnourished, worn out, and defeated:

A man herded about, surrounded by armed guards, starved and forced to live in filth loses his dignity; that is, he loses his valid position in regard to society, and consequently his whole ethics toward society . . .

California communities have used the old, old methods of dealing with such problems. The first method is to disbelieve it and vigorously to deny that there is a problem. The second is to deny local responsibility since the people are not permanent residents. And the third and silliest of all is to run the trouble over the county borders into another county.

He had no doubts as to the villians:

The Associated Farmers, which presumes to speak for the farms of California and which is made up of such earth-stained toilers as chain banks, public utilities, railroad companies, and those huge corporations called land companies—this financial organization in the face of the crisis is conducting Americanism meetings and bawling about Reds and foreign agitators. It has been invariably true in the past that when such a close-knit financial group as the Associated Farmers becomes excited about our ancient liberties and foreign agitators, someone is about to lose something. A wage cut has invariably followed such a campaign of Americanism.

Steinbeck quoted an Imperial Valley politician who said the farmers had a better way of dealing with labor problems than legal ones:

"The better way," as accepted by the large growers of the Imperial Valley, includes a system of terrorism that would be unusual in the Facist nations of the world. The stupid policy of the large grower and the absentee speculative farmer in California has accomplished nothing but unrest, tension, and hatred . . .if the terrorism and reduction of human rights, the floggings, murder by deputies, kidnappings, and refusal of trial by jury are necessary to our economic security, it is further submitted that California democracy is rapidly dwindling away.

He summed up:

John Steinbeck

The new migrants to California from the Dust Bowl are here to stay. They are of the best American stock, intelligent, resourceful, and, if given a chance, socially responsible. To attempt to force them into a peonage of starvation and intimidated despair will be unsuccessful. They can be citizens of the highest type, or they can be an army driven by suffering and hatred to take what they need. On their future treatment will depend which course they will be forced to take.

Considering the climate of the times, it took considerable courage to write the series and a commensurate amount to publish it.

One ironic consequence of the series was that Steinbeck heard that some migrants were upset about the use of the word "gypsies," which they considered pejorative; so he wrote a letter to the editor of the paper:

I have heard that a number of migrant workers have resented the title of the series of articles "Harvest Gypsies." The title was used ironically, since it is ironical that a huge group of workers should, through the injustice and bad planning of our agricultural system, be forced into a gypsy life. Certainly I had no intention of insulting a people who are already insulted beyond endurance.

The migrants at Weedpatch responded by sending Steinbeck a stuffed rag dog as a memento—"to migrant John."

That November, another significant event occurred: A roaring fire swept Cannery Row, destroying a good deal of it. One of the casualties was Ed Ricketts' lab; specimens and equipment could be replaced easily, but not Ed's library of books on marine biology, which he reckoned as one of the best outside a university, and valued at $2,000. It was a shattering blow, and Ed's business never really recovered from the loss.

Life was becoming more hectic for Steinbeck at this time; first the publication of his newspaper series, then the announcement that the Commonwealth Club of California had awarded him another gold medal, for *In Dubious Battle,* brought him very much to the attention of the public all over again. They tramped onto his property, peeked and poked around, broke the lock on the gate and knocked on his door, and wrote letters by the bagful. Work went badly on the new novel, and the Steinbecks yearned to take a break and get away; but they weren't sure they could afford it, with the prospect of a long spell ahead before the next publication. "I guess we'll have to pull in our horns financially," Steinbeck wrote to a friend. "I don't expect the little book *Of Mice and Men* to make any money. It's such a simple little thing."

A few days after he wrote this letter, the book was selected by the Book-of-the-Month Club, and it would become a bestseller immediately upon publication; within a month it had sold more than 100,000 copies.

10
THE MOVING
TARGET

STEINBECK'S THIRTY-FIFTH
birthday was a happy one, despite the difficulties he was having
with the new novel (or perhaps because of them to an extent – he
needed and wanted the striving and always expressed a fear that if
he reached a peak with his work, it might end, like a stream drying up).

With the success of *Of Mice and Men,* Steinbeck had staked out
rural California as his own literary territory, but the messages he
was sending, and their implications, were not always heeded by the
East Coast literary establishment, which had its ears to its own native ground and noses in the air to catch the breezes from Europe – a
posture as traditional as it is uncomfortable. He was criticized for his
language (too crude), and his characters (dimwitted lowlifes). All
these alleged flaws were apparent in his "simple little book."

The story is familiar enough not to need retelling, but its very
familiarity may have the effect of dimming the fact that it is one of
Steinbeck's most carefully written books, drawing as much of its considerable power from the way it is written as from what happens in
the story itself.

To begin with, although the story is often thought of as sentimental, it is in fact quite objective, even mechanistic, with no ser-

monizing or other indication of the author's point of view; the story is simply "something that happened," and in killing Lennie at the end, George is simply doing what he has to do.

Allegorically, the novel continues the theme of *In Dubious Battle,* as George and Lennie dream of a paradise—a place of their own, with rabbits and chickens—that will forever be lost to them. The story is set in Soledad, which of course is a real town, but the name means "loneliness" in Spanish. "Guys like us," George says in a continuing refrain, "that work on ranches, are the loneliest guys in the world . . ." In the course of the story, Steinbeck shows poignantly how and why it will always be that way, especially for the innocents who dare to dream.

Annie Laurie Williams, who handled the theatrical side of the agency, was a shrewd agent, as she proved by her handling of the manuscript. She showed the novel to Beatrice Kaufman, who was the East Coast representative for Samuel Goldwyn and, more importantly, the wife of famous playwright-director George S. Kaufman. The latter began reading it with mild interest, but before he was through he had already decided to direct it himself on Broadway.

Kaufman was even more of an antithesis to Steinbeck than John O'Hara had been; he was the epitome of the fast-talking, wisecracking New York Jewish intellectual, master of the cutting one-liner (when he heard that Steinbeck's dog had chewed up the manuscript, he remarked, "That dog must be a hell of an editor"). The only thing the two had in common, besides being heavy smokers, was that they both liked to work. Kaufman wrote Steinbeck immediately with some suggestions, mainly to do with strengthening the part of Curly's wife, and adding some humor to the bunkhouse banter to heighten the impending tragedy; Steinbeck took his advice. The play was scheduled for an autumn production on Broadway.

John and Carol decided to get away from California for a while and finally go to Europe. They booked passage on a ship—always his favorite form of travel—and sailed for New York on March 23. Steinbeck begged his agents to keep his arrival secret ("This ballyhoo is driving me nuts"), but Kaufman and O'Hara couldn't resist trying to show them the town and show them off. One dinner party was enough for Steinbeck ("I simply cannot write books if a con-sciousness of self is thrust on me"), and they sailed for Europe much relieved, leaving Kaufman a draft of the story in play form. They arrived in Sweden in May and after a few weeks went on to Russia —Steinbeck still had no taste for high-living foreign cities like Paris or London.

A few days after they sailed from New York, a curious event occurred, one that attracted little notice and that has gone unre-marked over the years—*Of Mice and Men* had its world premiere in San Francisco.

It is something of a mystery as to why Steinbeck would con-sent to have the show go on while he was half a world away; nor-mally an author wants to see how the work plays and hopes to hear some applause at the same time. One clue may lie in a letter to his agents, written in late March; in it, he says that he was recognized in San Francisco, presumably on the street by a stranger, and that "it made me sick to my stomach . . . Unless I can stand in a crowd without any self-consciousness and watch things from an unedito-rialized point of view, I'm going to have a hell of a hard time." He may well have been having actors at the San Francisco Theater Union read his story aloud while he worked on the script and given them permission to perform it in return. It ran for several weekends after its premiere on May 21, 1937, at the Green Street Playhouse in North Beach, only a few blocks from the speakeasy he had visited as a Stanford student during Prohibition.

STEINBECK WAS STILL

thinking about his phalanx theory, which was one thing that had drawn him to Russia, where all of society seemed to be a phalanx; but he was disappointed by it and soon returned to Sweden, where he had friends. He and Carol came back to the United States in August.

Upon their return, Covici published *The Red Pony,* made up of the two stories about Jody and his pony originally published in *North American Review,* with another added, titled "The Promise," which also features Jody and his family. Steinbeck was angry when he saw that it was to be a limited edition, finely printed and bound, selling for ten dollars; he expected to be crucified for commercialism. Instead, the offering was oversubscribed, to his amazement. "I didn't think there were that many damn fools in the world – with ten bucks, I mean," he wrote.

New York was sweltering and humid; so Kaufman invited John and Carol to his home in cool and pastoral Bucks County, Pennsylvania, where they could work on the script. There wasn't all that much to do, mostly fine-tuning; Kaufman enjoyed the give-and-take of communal work, but Steinbeck couldn't wait to get it over with. Back in New York, he sat through the conferences with Kaufman and producer Sam Harris and the set designer, and he sat through casting sessions dutifully; but as soon as all that was done, he left, saying merely that he felt everything was in good hands and his presence was no longer necessary. In reality, he felt uncomfortably out of his element and was dying to get home to work on the migrant-workers novel. Kaufman was shocked and dismayed, and he wouldn't speak to Steinbeck for years afterward.

John and Carol went to Chicago, where they bought a car and a new dog and then drove home (the pup was shipped later). Part of their trip took them along the same route the migrants were traveling to get to the Promised Land – Route 66. In years to come, a myth grew up about Steinbeck traveling with the Okies which he did nothing to refute, but in fact he and Carol traveled comfortably and by themselves. He did remember, however, details of the roadways, which came in handy later.

Back at home, Steinbeck decided to return to the source. The situation of the migrant workers had grown worse, with no end of misery in sight for them. He outfitted an old pie wagon into something roughly resembling a camper and set out for Gridley, where he again hooked up with Tom Collins. He quite sensibly feared for his safety and reputation and traveled incognito. Collins wangled a month's leave time to escort him, and they traveled the length of the great Central Valley, down to Arvin, and possibly into the Imperial Valley. They talked and listened to the migrants along the way, ate with them, and perhaps even worked with them. In this kind of close contact, Steinbeck could easily see that satire was not the best way to tell their story, that a detailed documentary method was needed. He went to work as soon as he returned home.

The outside world intruded a great deal that winter, however. *Of Mice and Men* opened on Broadway on November 23, starring

Wallace Ford as George, Broderick Crawford as Lennie, and Claire Luce as Curly's Wife, and it was a hit, running for 207 performances and winning the New York Drama Critics' Circle Award for best play. Pat Covici sent Steinbeck telegrams between the acts on opening night, telling him it was a great success, and his agents called immediately after the show to tell him the news; he finally admitted that he'd known that this was the big day, and been loopy with stage fright. Joseph Henry Jackson collected the reviews through the *San Francisco Chronicle,* and Steinbeck confessed that he was pleased that they were all favorable ("The critics didn't take pot shots at it as I thoroughly expected them to"). He celebrated by buying a new typewriter.

Broadway beckoned again a week later. Jack Kirkland, who had adapted Erskine Caldwell's *Tobacco Road* into what would become one of the longest-running plays in the history of the American theater, had optioned *Tortilla Flat* and now sent Steinbeck a script. Although Steinbeck wrote him a gracious letter praising it, he also attached a long list of criticisms. As he reread the script over the next week, it seemed to get worse and worse, and Steinbeck fired off letters and a telegram, trying to get Kirkland to come to California and work with him on it. He even wrote some scenes to show Kirkland how to get the right tone and feeling into them, but it was hopeless (as it probably would have been anyway, even in the hands of a more skilled dramatist). Carol went to New York for the opening on January 12, 1938; the show lasted four performances after being thoroughly savaged by the critics, who at least held Steinbeck blameless—there was a great deal to dislike about the production, which seems miserable in every respect.

Another irritant for Steinbeck was Hollywood. Agents and movie producers began calling, offering him large sums of money to come to work for the movies; they couldn't understand his refusals and persisted, simply raising the ante. To make matters worse for Steinbeck, he had no phone, and so had to walk all the way into town to return the calls and say no. "I have never before come in contact with anyone to whom the word no had no meaning whatever but these seem to be people like that," he wrote to his agents.

He still got a lot of unsolicited mail, but now there was an awful added element—begging letters. He wrote Joseph Henry Jackson:

CAROL STEINBECK.

John Steinbeck

I get sadder and sadder. The requests and demands for money pour in. It is perfectly awful. WPA worker in pencil from Illinois – "you have got luck and I got no luck. My boy needs a hundderd dollar operation. Please send a hundderd dollars. I will pay it back." That sort of thing. Getting worse every day. Maybe Cuernavaca isn't so far off at that if this doesn't die down. "Liberal negro school going to close if money isn't forthcoming. Can you stand by and see this school close after fifteen years?" Someone told a Salinas ladies' club that I had made three hundred thousand dollars this year. It is driving me crazy. "If you will just send me a railroad ticket to Boise I can come to California and get rid of my rheumatism." They're nightmarish . . . The damn things haunt me.

And to top it off, he was awarded another distinction of celebrity – he was hit with a paternity suit.

The Steinbecks' marriage had its tensions, like every other, and their early Bohemian lifestyle occasioned a certain amount of gossip, which you can still hear repeated today in Salinas and Monterey. Certainly John liked to drink and talk and hang out in bars – he was no saint, as he would be the first to admit. But above all, he liked to work, and he and Carol were a good team. He told her of the charge immediately and set out to fight it. The girl was local, not a tramp, and he did know her, which made the whole business quite painful for him. She was probably only looking for money, like the desperate people writing begging letters, but he was innocent and wouldn't settle.

In the end, Steinbeck's childhood illness provided him with an ace in the hole – the girl had no knowledge of the terrible scar left on his chest when his rib was removed to save his life, a scar that was impossible to miss. After some skirmishing with her attorney, the suit was dropped. Now he was free to pull together the enormous mass of notes on the migrants and turn them into a novel. Carol was given the job of reading the mail and discarding most of it, and of answering the newly installed telephone to tell people that Mr. Steinbeck was out of town.

II
DUSTED OFF AND
BURNED OUT

CALIFORNIA AGRICULTURE

has for most of its history been the domain of large landholders. The pattern was set with the establishment of the Spanish land grants and continued when they were taken over by the robber barons who owned the banks, mines, and railroads. As early as 1850, according to Josiah Royce, settlers were dismayed to find millions of acres of prime farmland lying fallow under absentee ownership. Some became squatters and farmed the land anyway; when threatened with eviction, hundreds of them marched on Sacramento to make their case. The brief insurrection was broken up by the National Guard, and the squatters were evicted from their farms. They became the first migrant workers.

Wheat was the big California crop then. It could be farmed on a large scale using mechanized methods, and within a few decades the state was the second-largest producer of wheat in the coutry. But in the 1870s the bottom fell out of California's overheated economy, and the price of wheat dropped precipitously. Fruits and vegetables were the answer; new railroad lines could carry them to market quickly, and California's climate guaranteed a variety of crops.

John Steinbeck

Fruits and vegetables, however, required more labor. The ex-squatters, Civil War veterans, and casualties of the long recession of the "terrible seventies" who made up the tramp labor force weren't enough. Another pattern was set: immigrant labor. The first group was the Chinese. Many were already in place and out of work after the completion of the major railroad lines, and they willingly went to work in the fields; most importantly, they worked cheap. The situation was ideal for the growers for a long time (there is some evidence that the Chinese even taught the growers much about raising various crops), but anti-Chinese feeling was growing in the cities, discriminatory laws were being passed with increasing frequency, and the violence against them spread from San Francisco and other cities out into the fields, in bloody and widespread vigilante action. The war cry was "The Chinese must go!" They did.

The benefits of alien labor were not lost on growers, however; after a few years of difficulties with bringing in the crops, they began quietly importing Japanese. There were some difficulties with the Japanese eventually, in that they saved their money, bought land, and went into competition with their former employers, and they also tended to organize and demand higher wages. This would not do.

Hindus from East India were a solution for a while; but the quality of their work wasn't as good, and they didn't go away between harvests, as the Orientals had. Mexicans were a good solution for a long time; but they, too, attempted to organize for better working conditions in the late twenties, and many had to be deported before their efforts were curtailed, which disrupted some harvests. Filipinos seemed to provide an alternative, but tended also to try to organize and, since they were American nationals, were more troublesome to get rid of (although at least, like all the others, they couldn't vote, which put limits on their trouble-making abilities).

Much of the unrest, misery, sickness, and poverty that underlie this brief account went largely unnoticed by the settled middle class of California and the rest of the nation, which had its own troubles with economic upheavals and, it should be noted, displaced persons and migrant labor. But California was a special case—its bright sun had darker shadows. Karl Marx wrote to a friend in 1880: "California is very important for me because nowhere else has the upheaval most shamelessly caused by capitalist centralization taken place with such speed." Fifty years later, the shame was hideously worse.

In 1933 the migrations from the Dust Bowl began, with farmers who had been "burned out, blown out, eaten out" of their homes and land. By early 1938, as Steinbeck sat down to yet another draft of his novel, more than 200,000 of these people, derisively known as "Okies" or "Arkies," were roving the state, looking for work, sick and tired and desperate, living in subhuman conditions.

Up until 1933, the migrant workers had largely been men, mostly brown and yellow foreigners, or a few white hoboes romanticized into "knights of the open road." Speeches about them by growers and politicians are filled with the casual racism of the time, and most citizens didn't get too upset about people beating on them. But suddenly the complexion of the migrants literally changed—they were white, American, and traveled as families. They were also here to stay. They couldn't be deported, and they might get to vote. As their numbers began to swell, they scared the hell out of the authorities.

It had long been the custom of the growers to advertise widely for labor before the harvest, often overstating the numbers needed. When the pickers would arrive, many more of them than were necessary, and usually without the means to move on, they'd be offered the lowest possible wages, which they had little choice but to accept. (In the years between the mid-twenties and thirties, wages actually went down, while agriculture thrived.)

Squalor is too good a word for the migrants' living conditions; they lived in the wild, under torn and tattered tents, washing in filthy irrigation ditches. When their jobs were done, they were often given a full tank of gas, so that they'd move on and become another county's problem. Growers and the state government did little for them and blocked the efforts of the federal government to improve their sorry lot.

All this Steinbeck attempted to set down in a novel. He had seen more than enough suffering in 1936 and 1937, in his trips with Tom Collins, but he couldn't stay away and was compelled to try to do something about the terrible situation. In the beginning of 1938, it poured down rain for weeks on end, adding even more to the migrants' misery, and Steinbeck went out to the San Joaquin Valley hoping to do some more newspaper articles, to expose the situation and shame the state into taking some action. He was offered commissions from *Life* and *Fortune* magazines, but turned down the latter. His deal with *Life* was that they would purchase food and medicine for the migrants instead of paying him a fee if they used the story (which they didn't although they printed the photos when *The Grapes of Wrath* was published the following year).

The tragedy Steinbeck found in the valley was worse than he had heard, and even more unnecessary than usual, since it was a virtual replay of a disaster that had occurred in the previous autumn, when growers had over-advertised for labor and left thousands stranded in the rain. On his return, he wrote to Elizabeth Otis: "The water is a foot deep in the tents and the children are up on the beds and there is no food and no fire, and the county has taken off all the nurses because 'the problem is so great we can't do anything about it' . . . It is the most heartbreaking thing in the world."

He poured his indignation onto the pages of the novel, still called *L'Affaire Lettuceberg,* and finished it by May: "It is a mean,

Tom Collins at "Weedpatch" – this is the best of
THE MIGRANT CAMPS.

nasty book and if I could make it nastier I would," he wrote Elizabeth Otis.

Around this time, his articles on the migrants were reproduced in a pamphlet entitled *Their Blood is Strong;* all the proceeds were to go to their aid ("I simply can't make money on these people," he said). Perhaps, rereading them, he thought twice about his bitter novel, for he abandoned it without showing it to his agent or publisher and started all over again.

The new effort was more realistic, meant to have the feel of a documentary. In this he was undoubtedly influenced by the work of filmmaker Pare Lorentz, noted for such works as *The River* and *The Plow That Broke the Plains,* which combine stark photography and poetic narration to stunning effect, similar to the way in which Steinbeck alternated journalistic episodes with the Joads' story. Having poured his bile into *L'Affaire Lettuceberg,* Steinbeck proceeded on the new book with a peaceful, steady purposefulness – he knew he had it now. "This is a very happy time," he wrote Elizabeth Otis. "It is a nice thing to be working and believing in my work again . . . I only feel whole and well when it is this way."

INTRUSIONS AND

perturbations there were, however. A developer had bought the acreage surrounding Garlic Gulch, subdivided it, and was building houses on it; so the Steinbecks found another place, this one of fifty acres, about three miles away, farther up in the Santa Cruz Mountains. It is ironic that, although Steinbeck was then financially well off, he refused to think so, and when he heard that his publisher was going bankrupt, he halted the negotiations on buying the property.

Pascal Covici was probably never meant to be a publisher – he liked to spend money too much, especially on authors. He had begun as publisher of fine books in limited editions, and he carried some of his feelings about fine bookmaking into his mainstream business, hiring good illustrators and designers and spending lavishly on advertising and promotion. He was normally overextended and, like many publishers, owed his printer a lot of money. When that gentleman called in his notes, Covici was through as a publisher. Ironically, Steinbeck's next book was the straw that broke the printer's back.

Covici believed in keeping his authors in the public eye, and it had been a while since there was a new Steinbeck book. He had pa-

---

John Steinbeck

pered over the gap with *The Red Pony*, but now he persuaded Steinbeck to let him publish a collection of his short stories—*Esquire* had
just bought some they had rejected years before, and that seemed
enough proof that there was a demand. So Steinbeck gathered the
original manuscripts, by then shopworn and somewhat the worse
for wear, and sent them off. When the printer saw them, he assumed
that Covici was trying to put one over on him—he is said to have
shouted, "Look at these filthy pages! It is obvious that this book has
been turned down by every publisher in the country!" A meeting of
the creditors of Covici-Friede was summarily held, and the company
was dissolved.

Covici was promptly hired by Harold Guinzburg of Viking
Press, another great editor, and he took Steinbeck with him. Other
publishers were lined up to sign him, but Steinbeck stayed loyal to
his friend. The book was issued shortly thereafter as *The Long Valley*. It was a success, selling 30,000 copies, and many of the stories
were anthologized over the years; though they vary in setting,
mood, theme, and style, most of them are among his best work.
The critical response was somewhat lukewarm, as it frequently is
with this kind of retrospective collection—the feeling seems to
have been that there was nothing new here.

Mainly, it gave Steinbeck the confidence to go ahead and buy
the fifty acres and build a new house on it. At about the same time,
Carol came up with a title for the novel—*The Grapes of Wrath*—and
started typing it, even as he scribbled to stay ahead of her. Steinbeck was convinced it wouldn't be a popular book and advised
Covici not to print a lot of copies, a prospect he faced with rueful
cheer. The book—an enormous manuscript—was finished in October and was promptly mailed off to his agent.

Steinbeck was exhausted, with terrible back pains and
neuritis, but a social duty called, in the person of Charlie Chaplin.
The two men had met when Steinbeck was in Hollywood for meetings on the filming of *Of Mice and Men*, and, as he had with Pare
Lorentz, Steinbeck made an immediate friendship with the little
comedian. Chaplin professed to envy Steinbeck's country life and
visited him several times, but in 1938 there was another reason—he
wanted to get in on a California vintage.

Shortly after Steinbeck moved to Los Gatos, he had become ac-
quainted with his neighbor up the hill, the iconoclastic and idio-

syncratic winemaker Martin Ray, a genuine character (the area abounded with them—even farther up the hill lived Paul Masson, every bit as colorful an individual). Ray's widow, Eleanor, recently recalled the visit of Steinbeck and Chaplin to their vineyard:

Charlie actually had a serious interest in winegrowing. He'd visited vineyards all over the world. He arrived on the mountain with Steinbeck one October morning, quickly donned overalls, and pitched in, pouring box after box of Chardonnay into the crusher. John Steinbeck, with his bad back, had to avoid hard work but managed to be in on everything. It was one astounding sight for Martin Ray, seeing the celebrated Chaplin hoisting heavy timbers onto the grape-must in the basket-press, then swinging on the press-handle vigorously with the others, even taking a hand enthusiastically at punching down the fermenting Pinot Noir.

Eleanor Ray recalls that after the grapes were crushed, Chaplin insisted on being the one to roast a turkey on the spit, played his accordian, and sang until the wee hours. Martin Ray put aside several barrels, reserved for Charlie, from the vintage. It was undoubtedly a wonderful way for Steinbeck to celebrate finishing his novel.

 Problems with the book were not long in coming. The language of the characters was considered too rough, and the ending, where Rose of Sharon, after bearing a stillborn child, offers her breast to a starving stranger, was deeply shocking for that time. Elizabeth Otis, a monument of tact, traveled to California to visit with John and Carol, during which time she persuaded Steinbeck to tone down the language, though he was adamant about the ending. They worked together, he flat on his back and in pain, she at a desk, negotiating every cuss word and barnyard epithet, coming up with substitutions and modifiers. When they were done, Otis attempted to send the changes to New York by way of Western Union, but the outraged operator refused to send such language at first. The agent somehow persuaded her; perhaps the negotiation was easier than the one she'd been through with Steinbeck.

 Covici wrote to say that he had read the book, that it had left him emotionally exhausted, and that Viking considered it the most important novel on their list, but asked Steinbeck to change the ending. Steinbeck refused at length: "I cannot change that ending. It is casual—there is no fruity climax, it is not more important than any other part of the book—if there is a symbol, it is a survival sym-

---

John Steinbeck

bol not a love symbol, it must be an accident, it must be a stranger, it must be quick . . . The fact that the Joads don't know him, don't care about him, have no ties to him—that is the emphasis. The giving of the breast has no more sentiment than the giving of a piece of bread." He added: "I am not writing a satisfying story. I've done my damndest to rip a reader's nerves to rags, I don't want him satisfied. And still one more thing—I tried to write this book the way lives are being lived, not the way books are being written."

The ending stayed.

12
IN THE PUBLIC DOMAIN

IN THE EARLY SPRING OF
1939, Steinbeck was physically and emotionally wracked and spent.
He endured six weeks of agonizing pain from his back before he
visited an osteopath, who helped but couldn't cure what became
chronic sciatica; he had his tonsils removed after discovering that
they were infected and poisoning his system; and he reached out, in
a flurry of letters, to old friends he hadn't seen in some time – Duke
Sheffield, Carl Wilhelmson, and Joseph Henry Jackson. When he
was better, he began going down to Monterey to visit Toby Street
and Ed Ricketts and took to puttering around the lab again.

The publication of *The Grapes of Wrath* in mid-April let loose a
flood of publicity, controversy, and adulation that elevated it to the
status of a national event and thoroughly overshadowed its
existence as a literary work. Within a month of its publication, more
than 80,000 copies had been sold, and by the end of the year, sales
had topped 430,000 copies, making it the second-best-selling novel
to date in America (the first was *Gone With the Wind*). It stayed on
the best-selling list into the following year. (In 1982, the *New York
Times* reported that it was the second-best-selling novel ever in
paperback in America, with 14,600,000 copies printed.) After the
reviews came editorials and stories about the controversy, then stories about the stories; Jack Benny joked about it on his radio show,

Eleanor Roosevelt approved of it in her newspaper column, West-brook Pegler condemned it in his, politicians damned him and had the book banned and stories were written about that. On the few occasions when Steinbeck responded, he made headlines; so he withdrew. Few authors, even in these days of television and celebri-ty-mongering magazines, have ever been so thoroughly in the news: John Steinbeck had, irrevocably, entered the public domain. He fought it, and lost, and it was his undoing.

The book quite muddled literary critics, especially in New York; to say that the reviews were mixed is to seriously understate the case. Burton Rascoe, in *Newsweek*, said the book had aspects that were "beautiful and even magnificent" but then complained about the structure, theme, and language: a "mass of silly propaganda, superficial observation, careless infidelity to the proper use of idiom, tasteless pornographical and scatological talk . . ."

Randolph Bartlett, in the *New York Times*, was less equivocal: "The one flaw in all of Steinbeck's work has been an obsession for the vulgar, the obscene and the lascivious . . . The more degraded phases of human conduct have their place in literature, but their use must always be governed by control, proportion and good taste." The Sunday reviewer for the *Times*, not so fastidious, raved about the book and somewhat restored the balance. Many other critics praised and damned it in the same review. One of the most influential, John Chamberlain, in *Harper's*, had spent some time on the road in California, and he wrote a sensible, sympathetic piece. The critic for the *Daily Worker* wrote a rave review, though not for its literary merit.

Steinbeck's friend Joseph Henry Jackson wrote a review in the *New York Herald Tribune* and managed in his long article not only to put the book and the struggle of "America's new dispossessed" in perspective, but to serve notice on the Eastern critics that it was the occasion for taking the author seriously at last.

Which was a little like suggesting that people notice a magnificent sunset in the midst of a forest fire. Six months after the publication of *The Grapes of Wrath*, when sales of the book were ac-tually increasing, having exceeded 200,000 copies, *Commonwealth* magazine said, "When a book sells like that, and when it causes the comment and controversy this book has, it becomes a cultural phe-nomenon of important dimensions. The literary and critical industry of the country is not really geared to handle it. The number of genuine ideas expressed in connection with the novel are humiliatingly few."

But the reviews were as nothing compared with the howls of outrage from the agricultural community and politicians, especially in Oklahoma and California. Steinbeck was attacked in both legislatures and in the granges and was warned by a friendly undersheriff that the Associated Farmers was going to try to set him up for trouble with a phony rape charge.

The conservative press came out swinging, especially the Hearst papers. The *San Francisco Examiner,* reporting on a pro-grower meeting sponsored by a new group called "Pro-America," thundered: "Distinguished and loyal Californians dipped the cloth to wipe some mud off the face of their state. These men and women who really know California broadcast facts in indignant answer to recent destructive fiction that has painted a lurid picture of their homeland." At the meeting, it was announced that a full-dress refutation was forthcoming, and indeed sometime later a book entitled *The Grapes of Gladness* appeared painting an unctuously rosy picture of farm life and happy migrants.

National publications also had their day. *Collier's* magazine (for which, ironically, Steinbeck later wrote) said the book was "propaganda for the idea that we ought to trade our system for the Russian system." *Look* magazine published pictures of the head of the Associated Farmers burning a copy of the book.

And of course it was banned, in several states, although it was a best-seller in Oklahoma, where the Tulsa Public Library had to stock twenty-eight copies to keep up with the demand. After a heated meeting in Bakersfield, California, it was removed from the Kern County library system and stayed banned for almost two years; a statewide effort by the Associated Farmers failed, however. The *Spartan Daily* reported that the San Jose Public Library didn't carry any of Steinbeck's works.

That June, Steinbeck let down his guard for a rare newspaper interview, although he refused to be photographed. He said, "I have always wondered why no author has survived a best-seller. Now I know. The publicity and fanfare are just as bad as they would be for a boxer. One gets self-conscious and that is the end of one's writing."

A movie was inevitable. Darryl Zanuck bought the rights for Twentieth Century-Fox and assembled a first-class team to film it —John Ford as the director, Nunnally Johnson the writer, Gregg Toland the cinematographer, and Alfred Newman the composer of the musical score. (*Look* magazine immediately did another feature, this time soliciting opinions on whether the movie should be made; prominent citizens, from Walter Winchell to the governor of California, said yes.)

Steinbeck was still getting offers to write for the movies, and was still refusing, but on his visits to Hollywood he found himself fascinated with both the movie medium and the place itself. He found that there were good, literate, and interesting people there —besides Chaplin and Pare Lorentz, he got to know and like Henry Fonda, Spencer Tracy (who had wanted to play both George in *Of Mice and Men* and Tom in *The Grapes of Wrath*), Burgess Meredith, and directors Lewis Milestone and King Vidor. He was also reunited with his boyhood friend Max Wagner, who was a struggling actor. The film colony was also fascinated with him, and provided him a comfortable environment—he was just one celebrity among many and was bothered much less there than anywhere else.

The life appealed less to Carol, who yearned to be back on their little ranch, and it led to an argument serious enough for Steinbeck to move into an apartment in Los Angeles, while she returned home. His back problems flared up again, and his socializing was restricted to visitors, most often Max Wagner, who one day brought along a pretty and vivacious actress-singer named Gwendolyn Conger; when Steinbeck recovered somewhat, the three of them went out on the town several times before he removed himself from temptation by returning to Los Gatos and normal life. In a few months, *The Grapes of Wrath* finally slipped to the number-two spot on the best-seller list, to his relief: "One nice thing to think of is the speed of obscurity," he wrote to Elizabeth Otis. "Grapes is not first now. In a month it will be off the list and in six months I'll be forgotten."

The book was dedicated to Carol, "who willed this book," and Tom (Collins, of course), "who lived it." At Steinbeck's insistence, all the lyrics of "The Battle Hymn of the Republic" were printed on the endpapers; he felt they were pertinent to the story, and rereading the words, one must agree.

For the allegorical underpinnings he so often used to enrich his novels, Steinbeck went to the Bible for *The Grapes of Wrath,* which accounts for the density and texture of the book, which begins with a drought and ends with a flood, details an exodus, and states a vision of salvation: "Use' ta be the fambly was first. It ain't so now. It's anybody. Worse off we get, the more we got to do."

In order to tell the whole story of the migrants, Steinbeck wrote sixteen interchapters that amplified and dramatized the context within which they were struggling, a device similar to the use of montage in film, and one that John Dos Passos had successfully used in several novels (Steinbeck acknowledged the literary debt). He was aware of the hazards of interrupting his narrative, and most of the interchapters add to or advance the action of the story line. It is a brilliant orchestration of technique and event, although it cost him some ground with several of the more fastidious Eastern literary critics; some felt it made the book uneven and unbalanced, while others thought he was merely showing off his versatility.

Few may have noticed that the group making the journey in the book consisted of twelve members of the Joad family and Jim Casy, the preacher, but most saw the parallels between Casy and John the Baptist and, later, Christ (although Christ-like attributes are given to Tom in the end, after Casy's death, with the "I'll be there" farewell speech). Most of the symbolism, including the controversial ending with Rose of Sharon (the Madonna) suckling a starving man, is not intrusive or overstated, except perhaps to a Bible scholar; it is well integrated into the narrative and into the characterizations, so that the people are never merely mouthpieces.

Unlike most of Steinbeck's work, this novel was firmly tied to real events, times, and places, and the controversy surrounding its publication seemed to ground it even more firmly in its times (in many ways, World War II ended the privations he described, at least for his group of migrants). After a while it was possible to accept *The Grapes of Wrath* as simply a great work of literature, and an enduring one at that.

ANOTHER NOTABLE BOOK

was published in 1939, though it provoked no controversy: *Between Pacific Tides,* by Edward F. Ricketts and Jack Calvin. It is a definitive sourcebook on marine life of the Pacific Coast, a careful and loving study of the ecology of the seashore. It had begun almost as a cottage industry among Rickett's circle, with Jack Calvin taking photographs and helping to make the scientific prose intelligible for the general reader, Ritchie Lovejoy doing the drawings, and just about everybody else helping to collect specimens. As a university press book, it made no significant money for Ricketts, which didn't matter to him a bit.

This cavalier attitude toward money had, however, brought Pacific Laboratories to the financial brink, and Ricketts had to acquire a partner, John Steinbeck, who loaned him $8,000 for a half-interest in the less-than-going concern. As Steinbeck spent more and more time at the lab, the two friends hatched a plan to do a book together. Steinbeck was happy again, as he always was at the prospect of work. He wrote Duke Sheffield, "I bought half the stock in Ed's lab which gives me equipment, a teacher, a library to work in." It also gave him a refuge from the increasing tensions in his marriage.

Things weren't helped by another trip to Los Angeles to see the completed films of *Of Mice and Men* and *The Grapes of Wrath*. Steinbeck apparently did not avoid the chance to see Gwen Conger again.

Of Mice and Men follows the play and novel quite closely and was shot in a simple, straightforward style, with no attempt to "open it up" for the movie screen. The film established Burgess Meredith as a movie star, if an offbeat one, and gave brief respectability to the acting career of Lon Chaney, Jr. It opened in December of 1939 and was a moderate success.

The Grapes of Wrath had been considerably reworked for the screen, but Steinbeck was pleased with it anyway, feeling that it was in many ways harsher than the book, as some of the pastoral descriptive material had been cut. In fact, although some of the book's power was blunted, it is a good dramatic adaptation. Nunnally Johnson, the screenwriter, was politically conservative, a classic Southern gentleman, but he was a true professional and awfully good at what he did. The troublesome ending was the first thing to go, and the screenplay ended with Tom's farewell speech to Ma; the trip to California was telescoped, and the storytelling pace generally speeded up. John Ford, who claimed never to have read the book, pretty much shot it as it was on the page.

The controlling intelligence behind the picture was Darryl Zanuck's; from the start, he wanted a documentary look and feel to the film, similar to the films of Lorentz and photos of Dorothea Lange. He supervised every aspect of production and, after the film was done, added the upbeat final scene of Ma Joad going on in hope ("We're the people!"), lifted from early in the book. He wrote and directed the scene himself, and it gave the film the solid, dramatic ending the book lacked, while reinforcing Steinbeck's theme that these were basically decent people here to stay.

Zanuck opened the film in New York in January 1940, orchestrated a masterful publicity campaign (he announced that the film would never be shown in California, then pretended to give in when thousands of letters protest swept in), had the movie's posters done by Thomas Hart Benton, and cleaned up at the box office. The film also made the National Board of Review's Ten Best List and won two Academy Awards.

In the midst of all the excitement, Steinbeck had not forgotten his source, Tom Collins. At Steinbeck's request, Collins had been hired as technical adviser and paid $15,000, a small fortune that brought his freedom from the increasingly frustrating work of fighting the bureaucracy of the Farm Security Administration.

That spring, Steinbeck won the Pulitzer Prize for *The Grapes of Wrath,* along with Carl Sandburg for *Abraham Lincoln: The War Years* and William Saroyan for the play *The Time of Your Life.* Steinbeck wrote to Joseph Henry Jackson, "While in the past I have sometimes been dubious about Pulitzer choices I am pleased and flattered to be chosen in a year when Sandburg and Saroyan were chosen. It is good company. That's the end of the quote. And it is one of the few times when tact and truth seem to be side by side."

13
KNIGHT
ERRANT

STEINBECK SPENT

increasing amounts of time in the winter of 1939 and spring of 1940 with Ed Ricketts, working hard, talking long, and recapturing the old days as they planned their collaboration on a book on marine biology. The idea of a serious nonfiction book lifted his spirits – "I can't tell you what all this means to me in happiness and energy," he wrote Duke Sheffield. "I was washed up and now I'm alive again, with work to be done and worth doing." He also thought such a book would subdue "this damnable popularity."

Steinbeck's letters of this period are reminiscent of the ones he wrote seven years earlier as he formulated his phalanx theory and rhapsodized about philosophical breakthroughs, showing again the influence of Ricketts, who drew him out and made him think and read and argue – and hope.

Like overaged Huck Finn and Tom Sawyer, they piled idea upon "what if" upon "why not," and then made it come true with a seventy-six-foot boat called the *Western Flyer*, a batch of bought, borrowed, and rented equipment, books, ninety cases of beer, and a plan – a cruise from Monterey down around the tip of Baja California and up and down the shores of the Sea of Cortez, collecting specimens, taking notes, and having a grand time doing all of it, away from telephones and begging letters and news of the war in Europe. The world seemed to be going to hell, and their solution was to say to hell with it for a bit.

They sailed early in March, with a crew of three and Carol; Toby Street had set up the charter and traveled with them as far as Los Angeles. They had quite an adventure for about six weeks, working and playing hard in that way that Steinbeck and Ricketts had so carefully cultivated. They collected thousands of specimens and eventually got a book out of the experience.

That didn't happen for a while, however, nor without friction between the two friends, for John and Carol went back to Mexico shortly afterward on another project—*The Forgotten Village*, Steinbeck's first screenplay. It was, at least, noncommercial. In Hollywood, he had met Herbert Kline and been impressed with documentaries Kline had made on the Spanish Civil War and the beginnings of World War II. He had invested in a Mexican film company with Kline in order to film a documentary about the Servicio Medical Rural, which attempted to bring modern medicine to the forgotten villages of the Mexican countryside. The film used nonactors, who

One way to get away from it all — the *Western Flyer*.

John Steinbeck

couldn't conform to the straitjacket demands of a script, and the weather wouldn't cooperate with the demands of the filmmakers; so Steinbeck's presence was needed to adapt and modify story situations as they went along, according to the day-to-day needs of the production.

Ricketts was annoyed at Steinbeck's defection from their project and drove down to Mexico, where he was at first welcomed, then avoided. Kline liked his lively interest and intelligent suggestions initially, but then a basic philosophical difference between Ricketts and Steinbeck became a vivid sore spot: Steinbeck's story was propagandistic and preachy, advocating action, change, and hope, moving from examining "something that happened" to what seemed to Ricketts to be an attempt to make something happen; Steinbeck had moved from the cool, nonteleological observer to the passionate apostle. Ricketts, on the other hand, thought that if the social system (the ecology) were changed, many problems would solve themselves; he collected his thoughts on the matter in an "Anti-Script," which did not please Steinbeck, and took himself off to the library of the Mexican Academy of Sciences for further research on their book. In a curious way, it was a conflict reminiscent of the one between Jim and Doc in *In Dubious Battle,* a conflict that had always lurked beneath the surface of their friendship.

Steinbeck and Carol returned to Los Gatos in early summer, but he was soon on the move again; the time is marked by an increasing restlessness, which became his pattern. Steinbeck was discovering that there were pleasant aspects to his celebrity, which included an audience with the president of the United States. He had written to Franklin D. Roosevelt about the impending crisis in the Western Hemisphere, feeling that the Germans were winning the propaganda war in South America, and FDR saw him for twenty minutes at the White House. Later that summer, Steinbeck visited again (and also had a reunion with his uncle, Joe Hamilton, who had gotten him a job as a reporter in New York fourteen years before and had urged him to go into advertising—it must have been sweet).

He also went back to Mexico and stopped in Hollywood several times in all these comings and goings. His relationship with Gwen Conger had become an affair, which delighted and tormented him alternately. He was attempting, too, to get some of his other work filmed—anything, it seems, other than returning to the old, settled life at the ranch with Carol.

The filming of *The Forgotten Village* ended late in 1940, and postproduction work began in Hollywood early in 1941; *Tortilla Flat* was also being made and was released that year (it did nothing to enhance Steinbeck's reputation and is a classic example of a Hollywood-sanitized botch). Pat Covici, worried about the fact that more than a year had passed without publication of a book by Steinbeck, persuaded him to let Viking publish a book of 136 stills from *The Forgotten Village,* linked by the film's narration, which he reluctantly agreed to.

Steinbeck now began to write the book on the Sea of Cortez expedition, working from detailed notes kept by Ricketts and from the captain's log. Carol had been ill much of the winter with a dragged-out flu, and he persuaded her to go to Hawaii for two months while he began writing hard.

He was also thinking hard, and when Carol returned from the Islands, he confessed his affair with Gwen; Carol's furious response was that she was not going to give him a divorce. He moved out, back to Pacific Grove, and put the ranch on the market. Work continued on *Sea of Cortez: A Leisurely Journal of Travel and Research,* with the small satisfaction that if he could not have Carol out of his life, he could have her out of his work—she is never mentioned in the book as being on the trip.

The plan for the writing of *Sea of Cortez* had been laid out straightforwardly even before the *Western Flyer* had left the docks of Monterey the year before, but Steinbeck had made a hash of it most of the way; he was dilatory about writing on the trip, let celebrity and sexual misadventure distract him afterward, and now came to the job a little stale and very much strained. It didn't help his concentration when Gwen joined him in Pacific Grove.

At times, in the manuscript, Steinbeck stretched himself to write well and capture the feel of their adventure and all the beauties they found, and at times he barely converted the notes and captain's log into narrative; a few parts are all by Ricketts. Pat Covici was bemused, worried, and exhortative during this time, and when he got the manuscript, ambiguously supportive: "In my little life, which is about three-fourth done, you are my rarest experience. Take that with all its implications, cynically as well if you want to. The soul of man is not too simple; certainly not for me. What I do positively know is that I want you to go on."

The changes Steinbeck had made in his life and work, or had simply allowed to happen in some cases, had a profound effect, and quickly. The film of *The Forgotten Village* was held up because of a censorship battle over some of the scenes involving childbirth on screen, and the book was seen as a trifle that exploited the author's reputation. The unkindest cut of all came from Joseph Henry Jackson, who headlined his review "John Steinbeck Goes All Simple and Just Overdoes It." The review has savage passages, including one about "the curious, fatherly-godlike love that Steinbeck manifests for its characters" and the "chastiseth-whom-he-love attitude implicit in so much of Steinbeck's work," which sound more like the spleen of Eastern critics than the former champion of Steinbeck. The book is bad work and Jackson had a point, but the biliousness of the review may come from the fact that Jackson and his wife had spent a good deal of time with the Steinbecks, including their first Mexican trip, and that he was upset at John's now-public adultery and the humiliation of Carol.

Sea of Cortez fared better, but not much. Timing may have had something to do with it, as it was published two days before the bombing of Pearl Harbor, but the first printing was only 7,500 copies, the smallest for a Steinbeck book in several years. It attracted little attention among reviewers in the East, and Jackson had two others review it, one as a literary work (not terribly favorable) and the other (kindly) by Joel Hedgepeth, a biologist who worked at Hopkins Marine Station and who was a member of Ricketts' circle. There are those who claim that the book is crucial to understanding Steinbeck and his philosophy, and in truth it has a number of revealing passages and ruminations; but in general it is a distracted and somewhat oblique work, quite uneven—as one critic described it, "a cioppino of travel, biology and philosophy."

Muddles were constant that year. He and Gwen moved to New York after the manuscript of *Sea of Cortez* was finished, and he was plunged back into the nasty side of celebrity again, since Carol was also in New York; she had fled earlier, when Gwen came up to Pacific Grove to be with John. Now they were fuel for the newspapers' fires, and Carol seemed to relish the fight, adding to his discomfort—where before her pride had kept the situation

JOHN AND GWEN.

John Steinbeck

private, now it was a public scandal; knowing how much he'd hate it, she gave newspaper interviews and told how she was "fighting for her man." It was a futile gesture, as he did what he could only do now, guilty as hell – flee. He and Gwen moved around New York, first to the country home of Burgess Meredith and then to a small and unfashionable hotel in Manhattan. All the while, he was writing, a novel again, but as he was thinking of what a divorce was going to cost him, he also conceived it as a play, much as he had with *Of Mice and Men*.

Somewhere in his talks with Ed Ricketts in Mexico and later in Pacific Grove as they were pulling the manuscript of *Sea of Cortez* together, and in their worries about the war and the way the human race tears itself apart, he had conceived the idea for a non-teleological study of a town invaded and occupied by an army – what would be the "something that happened"? With the advent of World War II, the idea gained urgency and became more than an academic exercise.

The novel was *The Moon is Down,* and there seems to be no evidence that it ever went beyond a first draft before publication, although the play script was worked over by Lee Strasberg, the director. It was the only novel by Steinbeck not to be thoroughly rewritten, and the first not overseen by Carol, accepted without question by Covici. Perhaps the desire of his agents and editor to help him through his personal difficulties blinded them to its flaws, perhaps it was anti-Nazi fervor, but no one called Steinbeck's attention to its considerable shortcomings; the book was rushed into print early in 1942, followed soon after by the play. The novel was an immediate best-seller, the play was panned but drew audiences, and neither enhanced Steinbeck's reputation in the end. His lack of judgment on the unnamed oppressors (the Nazis), and the passivity of his theme that right would somehow prevail, seemed perversely obtuse and limp in the face of the rapidly unfolding horrors of the war.

Carol had returned to California and given up the fight. In March of 1942, she went to court in Monterey and filed suit for divorce, accompanied by Toby Street as her lawyer and Ed Ricketts as her witness; an interlocutory decree was granted immediately. Steinbeck did not return to oppose the action, which quite fairly granted her half of his assets to that point.

ALTHOUGH STEINBECK

came back to Monterey and Salinas for extended visits after World War II, and once fantasized about buying a ranch in the area, he never lived there again. He became something of a wanderer, an exile from his literary Eden; his writings about it then were, in the main, diffident, awkward, and clumsy. He had drawn his strength as an artist from his native soil and, like Antaeus of Greek myth, he had lost it when he left it.

John Steinbeck

EPILOGUE

IN LATE OCTOBER 1962,
Steinbeck turned on his television set and discovered that he had
won the Nobel Prize – only the fifth American to do so in sixty years
(the others were Sinclair Lewis, Eugene O'Neill, William Faulkner,
and Ernest Hemingway). The phone in his house on Long Island began to ring within minutes and rang all day. Although the Nobel
Prize is the subject of much deserved controversy, it is still the pin-
nacle, and Steinbeck was grateful and honored to be there.

The intervening twenty years since he left California had been
difficult ones for him as a writer, and only slightly less so as a man.
His marriage to Gwen was brief, producing two sons, much bitterness, and a divorce that left him broke. He had lost touch with many
old friends, and Ed Ricketts had died in an accident, his car rammed
by a train in the night. The pain was eventually more than mitigated
by his third wife, Elaine, who made him a happy marriage.

There was nothing Elaine could do for the work, however, except encourage him to keep at it, which by all accounts she did. He
wrote seven more novels, of which only *Cannery Row* (1944) and
East of Eden (1952) are worth more than passing interest, the former
because it captures life in Monterey with something like the old vig-

or and humor (although as an homage to Ed Ricketts, who is its hero, it was an odd tribute – it made Ricketts self-conscious and destroyed his privacy, and we know what Steinbeck thought about that). *East of Eden* was a conscious attempt to write a big book that captured his family and Salinas, but it ended up self-conscious and disjointed, with brilliant passages reflecting his nostalgia for the land and the Hamilton side of his family alternating with a parable of evil and the dark side of life that is turgid and confused; the portrait of his mother is sprightly and loving, but his father eluded him yet again. There was enough that was good in the book to somewhat restore his critical reputation, but he then flummoxed it with *Sweet Thursday,* a sequel to *Cannery Row* that attempted to lay Ricketts' ghost to rest with a happy ending for him, on paper at least.

Movies were made based on his work, and they generally dragged down his reputation, although the fault was never entirely his; two screenplays that he wrote himself and that turned out well were *The Red Pony* and the excellent, underrated *Viva Zapata!* He planned a television anthology of his stories, but nothing came of it, which is just as well, considering what the medium would have done to his message.

Irony was no stranger to Steinbeck, and a large helping came with the Nobel Prize, as *Travels with Charley* was published shortly afterward. This slight, second-rate book dramatized his plight as a writer past the peak of his powers; and the fact that it became an enormous best-seller only added to the irony and fed his detractors' anger.

For Steinbeck was, to a great extent, an unpopular choice for the prize. The critics' reaction was ferociously negative in many journals, bluntly summed up in the *New York Times* by Arthur Mizener, who headed his article "Does a Moral Vision of the Thirties Deserve a Nobel Prize?"

All of Steinbeck's early work returned to print with the award, and a new generation of readers had a chance to decide that question for themselves. Since most of the books remain in print, it seems that Mizener's question has been answered to the only extent that it can, or at least that matters. (And of course, the imminent struggle of Cesar Chavez and the United Farm Workers demonstrated that some moral visions should not be retired prematurely.) A writer writes for readers, after all, and in his best work John Steinbeck did for millions of them what every writer worth his salt wants and the best of them achieve. If what he accomplished did not bring him peace, that was a trade-off he had been willing to make all the way back to the lonely years at Lake Tahoe, and he made it without a whimper.

Steinbeck spent the next six years working on a modern-English version of his beloved *Le Morte d'Arthur,* and died in his sleep on December 20, 1968. He was buried in Salinas, California, home at last.

SELECTED BIBLIOG RAPHY

Astro, Richard. *Steinbeck and Ricketts: The Shaping of a Novelist*. Minne apolis: University of Minnesota Press, 1973.

Donohue, Agnes M., ed. *A Casebook on "The Grapes of Wrath."* New York: Thomas Y. Crowell Co., 1968.

Fensch, Thomas. *Steinbeck and Covici: The Story of a Friendship*. Middle burg, Vermont: Paul S. Ericksson, 1979.

French, Warren, ed. *A Companion to "The Grapes of Wrath."* New York: The Viking Press, 1963. (Contains text of "Their Blood Strong.")

Lisca, Peter. *John Steinbeck, Nature and Myth*. New York: Thomas Y. Crowell Co., 1978.

Lisca, Peter. *The Wide World of John Steinbeck*. New Brunswick: Rutgers University Press, 1958.

McWilliams, Carey. *Factories in the Field: The Story of Migratory Farm Labor in California*. Boston: Little, Brown & Co., 1939.

Ricketts, Edward F., and Calvin, Jack. *Between Pacific Tides*. Palo Alto: Stanford University Press, 1939.

Shasky, Florian J., and Riggs, Susan F., eds. *Letters to Elizabeth*. San Fran cisco: The Book Club of California, 1978. (Introduction by Carlton A. Sheffield.)

Steinbeck, Elaine, and Wallsten, Robert, eds. *Steinbeck: A Life in Letters.* New York: The Viking Press, 1975.

Tedlock, Ernest W., and Wicker, C.V., eds. *Steinbeck and His Critics: A Record of Twenty-Five Years.* Albuquerque: University of New Mexico Press, 1956.

Valjean, Nelson. *John Steinbeck, The Errant Knight.* San Francisco: Chronicle Books, 1975.

INDEX